SO-BAN-288

FAMILY DEVOTIONS
for Children

KENNETH N.
TAYLOR

Illustrations by Shelley Matheis

TYNDALE
KIDS

Visit Tyndale's exciting Web site at www.tyndale.com

Copyright © 1999 by Tyndale House Foundation. All rights reserved.

Illustrations copyright © 1999 by Shelley Matheis. All rights reserved.

Edited by Betty Free

Designed by Julie Chen

Scripture quotations on pages 4, 35–36, 45, 49, 53–54, 57, 89, 195, 202–203 are from *The Living Bible* copyright © 1971. Used by permission of Tyndale House Publishers, Inc., Wheaton, Illinois 60189. All rights reserved.

Scripture quotations on pages 39, 72–73, 77 are from *The Simplified Living Bible,* copyright © 1990. Used by permission of Tyndale House Publishers, Inc., Wheaton, Illinois 60189. All rights reserved.

All other Scripture quotations are taken from the *Holy Bible,* New Living Translation, copyright © 1996. Used by permission of Tyndale House Publishers, Inc., Wheaton, Illinois 60189. All rights reserved.

Library of Congress Cataloging-in-Publication Data

Taylor, Kenneth Nathaniel.
  Family devotions for children / Kenneth N. Taylor.
     p. cm.
  Summary: Presents Bible verses along with readings about everyday life and study questions to help young people come to know more about God.
  ISBN 0-8423-1122-X
  1. Children Prayer-books and devotions—English. 2. Family Prayer-books and devotions—English. [1. Prayer books and devotions.] I. Title.
BV4870.T33   1999
249—dc21   99-23921

Printed in the United States of America

05   04   03   02   01   00   99
7   6   5   4   3   2   1

Family Devotions for Children

Other Children's Books by Kenneth N. Taylor:

Right Choices
My Little Bible in Pictures
My First Bible in Pictures
My First Bible Words: A Kid's Devotional
Everything a Child Should Know about God
Almost 12
Stories about Jesus
My First Bible for Tots series
Family Time Bible in Pictures
Ken Taylor's Favorite Bible Stories
Good News for Little People
Wise Words for Little People
Big Thoughts for Little People
Giant Steps for Little People
The Bible in Pictures for Little Eyes (Moody Press)
Devotions for the Children's Hour (Moody Press)

CONTENTS

THE HOLY SPIRIT

THE CHURCH

GOD AND YOU

A Note to the Kids Who Read This Book

Hello from Grandfather Taylor. Perhaps you will be interested to know that I have 28 grandchildren! Some of them are about your age. I know from them how much fun you are probably having at school. Perhaps you are playing soccer and having fun in other ways too.

You are learning so much at school, at Sunday school and church, and also at devotion times with your family.

This book has been written for family devotions, but it is also for your use when you are by yourself or with your friends.

The book tells many things you need to know about God. You already know some of these things, but there may be parts of the book that will give you new knowledge that will be important to you for the rest of your life.

Blessings to you,

Ken Taylor

PART ONE

THE
BIBLE

A Letter from Heaven

KERI was very
happy when the mail carrier brought her a letter.
It was from her grandfather and grandmother,
and it said, "Happy Birthday, Keri!"

We all like to get letters. Have you ever
thought about what it would be like to get a letter from God? That would be wonderful!

Will it surprise you if I tell you that God has
sent you a letter? It didn't come in the mailbox,
and it is much bigger than an ordinary letter, for
it is a whole book. You've probably guessed that
I am talking about the Bible!

God gave us the Bible to tell us the way to

heaven and to tell about his plans for the world and for each of us. So you need to read part of this letter from God every day. It will tell you how to keep from doing things that anger God and how God himself is ready to help you be pure and honest. It will tell you about prayer—how to praise and thank God, as well as give him your requests. It will also tell about Jesus Christ, God's Son, who came from heaven to save us. It will teach you about his miracles, and how he died and came back to life again.

What a wonderful book the Bible is—how important it is to read some of it each day! It will keep you from sin and show you God's way for your life.

A BIBLE VERSE TO READ

> I have thought much about your words, and stored them in my heart so that they would hold me back from sin.   *Psalm 119:11*

SOME QUESTIONS TO ANSWER

1. When would be a good time each day for you to read something from the Bible? After school? At bedtime?
2. Can you memorize Psalm 119:11 together with your family? (See above.)

3. What does the verse say will happen when you memorize words from the Bible?

A PRAYER TO PRAY

Father in heaven, thank you for your letter. Help me to read some of it every day. Please help me to keep from sin and to be more and more the way you want me to be. Amen.

How Did God Write the Bible?

DID God use a computer or a pencil or a pen to write the Bible? No, that was not the way. He told many different people to write parts of his letter. He told them what to say, and they wrote it all down for us to read.

How did God tell the people what to write? Sometimes he sent them dreams. In their dreams God told them what he wanted his people to know and do. Then the writers wrote down what God told them. Sometimes God sent them visions. If they had a vision, that means they were sitting or standing somewhere and suddenly saw a picture in their mind. Then they wrote down what they saw. And sometimes God spoke with a voice just like you and I do when we talk to each other. Finally, all of the messages God gave to these people were put together in a book, the Bible.

What a wonderful book to have! How kind God was to write us this letter that tells us what he wants us to know and do.

Your pastor probably reads the Bible a lot, and that is one reason why he is such a good person. Yes, he can make mistakes. But when he reads the Bible, God helps him know what is right. God will help you, too, when you know what he wants. He tells you this in his letter to you, the Bible.

A BIBLE VERSE TO READ
> It was the Holy Spirit who moved the prophets to speak from God.   *2 Peter 1:21*

SOME QUESTIONS TO ANSWER
> 1. How did people who wrote the Bible know what God wanted them to write?
> 2. What is a vision?

SOME THINGS TO PRAY ABOUT

- ◆ Thank God for his letter to us.
- ◆ Thank God for your family.

PART TWO

THE
BEGINNING

God Made Everything

GOD lives in heaven, and he is powerful beyond our wildest imagination! He made the earth and stars and sun and everything else. A long time ago he made the animals and birds and plants. Then he made the first man and the first woman.

Think about some of the things in our beautiful world—the giraffe and the elephant and the lion and the trees. Imagine what it was like long,

13

long ago when there were no trees or animals anywhere in all the world. But then God made them. Who except God could do this?

Allison and her friend Melanie were talking about God.

"How do we know God made the world?" Melanie asked.

"Because," Allison said, "we can look around us and see the sky and trees and birds and animals. You and I could never make them. Only God could."

Think about how great God is to be able to make the sun and stars and birds and everything else! We can only draw pictures of these things—we can't make them. Only God can! He said, "Let there be . . ." and there it was! You or I could never make even a mouse or a puppy! But God can. He can do anything.

Light travels 186,000 miles every second. It travels fast enough to go around the entire world seven times between now and . . . now! Yet it takes eight minutes for light from the sun to arrive here on earth. That's because the sun is 93 million miles away from us! Look at the stars at night. They are so far away that it takes from thousands to millions of years for their light—at the speed of light—to come to us. God's power in making the sun and stars, and placing them in the heavens, is beyond understanding! And he is our God and Father.

A BIBLE VERSE TO READ

In the beginning God created the heavens and the earth.
Genesis 1:1

SOME QUESTIONS TO ANSWER

1. God made everything, and he made you. So you are hs. What are some things he wants you to do?
2. When you see the sunshine, how long ago did it leave the sun before you could see it?

SOME THINGS TO PRAY ABOUT

◆ Thank God for making the sun and stars.
◆ Thank him for your friends whose names are _____ and _____ and _____. You can pray for them now.

God Made the Angels

ONE day Matt and Sierra were reading in the Bible about angels. "What is an angel?" Sierra wanted to know. Matt didn't know the answer, so the children asked Pastor Winters. These are some of the things he told them.

Angels are different from people because they don't have bodies like we do. They are spirits, so we can't see them unless God sends them to talk to us. Then they usually look similar to the way we do.

God made the angels before he made the first man and woman. He made millions of angels. They live in heaven, where they worship and

praise God, but sometimes he sends them to earth as messengers or helpers.

The Bible tells how an angel helped a man named Daniel in the lions' den. The angel closed the lions' mouths so they could not hurt Daniel in any way.

Another time an angel named Gabriel brought a message from God to a young woman named Mary. Gabriel told her she had been chosen by God to be the mother of Jesus, our Savior. Mary was frightened at first because of what the angel said. But Gabriel told her not to be afraid. "God will bless you more than any other woman," the angel told her.

Sometimes when angels appear to people, the angels' clothing looks dazzling white. But we don't know if they have wings or not. Sometimes they appear to more than one person at the same time, as they did to the shepherds when baby Jesus was born.

The Bible says that an angel may come to help someone but then disappear before anyone knows it was an angel. So you may see an angel sometime and not realize it!

Other times God may send an angel to protect you, but you won't even see this helper. There is probably an angel in the room with you right now!

Matt and Sierra thanked Pastor Winters for telling them all about angels. Then Sierra asked, "When Christians die, do they become angels?"

"No, better than that!" said the pastor. "God has done something even better for us. He has adopted us into his family! God made the angels to be messengers and helpers, but he made you to become his very own child, whom he will love forever and ever."

A BIBLE VERSE TO READ

God calls his angels "messengers swift as the wind, and servants made of flaming fire."

Hebrews 1:7

SOME QUESTIONS TO ANSWER

1. How are angels different from people?
2. Name some ways that angels helped Bible-time people.
3. Can you think of a time when an angel may have protected you?

SOME THINGS TO PRAY ABOUT

- ◆ Thank God for making angels.
- ◆ Thank God for taking care of you and your friends.
- ◆ Praise God for making you even more special than angels!

The Bad Angels

WHEN God made the angels, they were all good. But God gave the angels minds so they could decide for themselves whether or not to love and obey him. At first thought it might seem very unlikely that they would turn against the wonderful, loving God who had created them. But they did. Now there are some bad angels, called demons or evil spirits.

Their leader, whose name is Satan, was once the greatest of the angels. God made him and gave him life along with all the other angels. But Satan, who is also called the devil, became proud. He wanted to be like God. He got many other angels on his side, and there was war in heaven. Satan and his evil angels fought against God and his good angels. And, of course, God's side won, for who can fight against God and win? So God threw Satan out of heaven along with all the other angels who were Satan's followers.

Now Satan is here with us on earth. Satan can go wherever he wants, but we can't see him. He and his evil angels find ways to get people to forget about God or to be against God.

I am sorry to say that some people have been so badly fooled by Satan that they do what he wants instead of what God wants. They may even worship him and pray to him instead of worshiping God. These people are being tricked by Satan. They meet together and ask Satan to help them. They are giving themselves to God's worst enemy. Stay away from people like that.

Satan is an evil angel, and no one should ever listen to him. He may try to make you think that wrong is right. Don't let him convince you. Don't worship him or talk to him. Don't talk to his evil angels, the demons, either. They only want to fool you and harm you by getting you to worship Satan instead of our Lord Jesus Christ, who is God.

Don't forget that Jesus is more powerful than

Satan. He can keep you safe from the devil and the other evil angels. Just trust Jesus and obey him. And remember how important it is to spend time with Jesus and with people who love him. Christians can encourage one another to keep following Jesus and not be tricked by Satan.

A BIBLE VERSE TO READ

> But when people keep on sinning, it shows they belong to the Devil, who has been sinning since the beginning. But the Son of God came to destroy these works of the Devil.   *1 John 3:8*

SOME QUESTIONS TO ANSWER

1. Is Satan a good angel or an evil angel?
2. What do we call Satan's evil angels?
3. How can you keep from being tricked by Satan?

SOME THINGS TO PRAY ABOUT

◆ Ask God to help you never to be fooled by Satan.
◆ Pray that you will love God more than anyone else.

God Wanted Friends

ONE night Rebecca and Jordan went outside with their father and mother. They looked up at the moon and the stars. "Have the stars always been there?" Rebecca asked.

"No," her father told her. "Once there were no stars anywhere. And no sun or moon or earth or people. There was only darkness—everywhere."

"Was God alive then?" Jordan wanted to know.

"Yes," his father told him. "God has always been alive, forever and ever!"

"How did the stars get there?" the children asked.

"One day God made them and put them there," Mother said. "Then he made the flowers and fish and all the animals. But God wanted friends who were like himself so he could talk to them. Then one day God wasn't lonely anymore."

"Why not?" the children asked.

"Because he made a man named Adam to be his friend and planted a wonderful garden called the Garden of Eden where Adam would live. God filled the Garden with beautiful trees. Many of them were fruit-bearing trees good for food. There was a river in the Garden too.

"The Lord God put Adam in the Garden to care for it. Then God said Adam should have someone to help him. So God brought the animals to Adam, but none was the right kind of help for him. So God did this wonderful thing: He put Adam to sleep and took part of his side—perhaps one of Adam's ribs—and made a woman. God made her to be a helper and companion for Adam. Adam named her Eve. How happy the first people were, and how happy God was to have them as his friends."

Do you know that God wants you to be his friend? And *he* wants to be *your* friend! Think about it: The God who made the whole world and all of the stars loves you! Amazing! Give your life to him, and always do whatever he tells you to. And because he loves you so much, ask him to help you love him, too.

SOME BIBLE VERSES TO READ

Then God said, "Let us make people in our image, to be like ourselves. They will be masters over all life—the fish in the sea, the birds in the sky, and all the livestock, wild animals, and small animals." So God created people in

his own image; God patterned them after
himself; male and female he created them.

Genesis 1:26-27

SOME QUESTIONS TO ANSWER
  1. What were the names of the first two
     people God made?
  2. How can you show that you love God?

A PRAYER TO PRAY
  Dear Lord, I am so glad that you love me.
  Now help me to love you and to give you my
  life so that I can bring you happiness. Amen.

God's Warning to Adam and Eve

WHEN God made Adam and planted the Garden of Eden, he planted the tree of life in the center of the Garden so that Adam could eat its fruit and live forever. God also planted the tree of the knowledge of good and evil, but he told Adam never to eat fruit of that tree or he would die.

God told Adam to care for the beautiful Garden and warned him not to eat the fruit from that particular tree. Adam could enjoy every other tree in the Garden, but he must stay away from the tree in the center of the Garden called the tree of the knowledge of good and evil.

God showed his love to Adam when he created Eve from Adam's side. God showed his love to both Adam and Eve when he gave them the ability to make choices.

God could have made Adam and Eve so that they had to obey him. But he didn't do that. He wanted them to have a choice. So instead of telling them they *had* to obey him, God let them know *how* to obey him. He lets *us* know how to obey him too. There are things God

tells us we must *not* do and other things that we *must* do. We must love God. This gives pleasure and joy to our heavenly Father. We must obey our parents. But we must not swear or use bad words or think bad thoughts. We must not steal. We must not lie. Those are some of God's rules, or commandments. If we obey them, God is pleased. And *we're* happy too because we're showing love to our Creator and doing what he created us to do!

SOME BIBLE VERSES TO READ

> The Lord God placed the man in the Garden of Eden to tend and care for it. But the Lord God gave him this warning: "You may freely eat any fruit in the garden except fruit from the tree of the knowledge of good and evil. If you eat of its fruit, you will surely die." *Genesis 2:15-17*

SOME QUESTIONS TO ANSWER

1. What tree did God tell Adam and Eve never to eat from?
2. What would happen to them if they did?
3. How do you make God happy? Have you ever made him sad?

A PRAYER TO PRAY

Dear God, you're my heavenly Father, and I want to please you. I don't want to make you sad. Help me to know what to do, and help me not to do things you say I shouldn't do. I want to make you glad. Amen.

Satan Tempts
Adam and Eve

WE HAVE already read that Satan had been the greatest of the angels. God had put him in charge of many other angels. But do you remember the awful thing that happened? Satan turned against God. He got some of the other angels to be on his side. Then there was war in heaven.

How foolish it was for Satan and his angels to fight against God. They were thrown out of heaven. Then they were very angry because they had lost the war against God. They wanted to get even with him.

This is what Satan decided to do to get even:

He decided to hurt God's friends Adam and Eve,
there in the Garden of Eden. But Satan knew
that God wouldn't let him hurt them unless
they disobeyed God. So Satan thought of a way
to get them to disobey. Through a crafty serpent
he visited Adam and Eve in the Garden of Eden.
He pretended that he was their friend and that
he wanted to help them. He told them to eat the
fruit from the tree in the middle of the garden
and said it wouldn't hurt them at all. He seemed
to be saying to them, "It will be good for you.
Don't listen to God. Don't pay any attention to
what he said."

I wish Adam and Eve hadn't listened to Satan
when he told them to disobey God! I wish they
had told him, "Get out of here, Satan. You are
God's enemy. You are not our friend." But do
you know what happened?

I am sorry to tell you what Adam and Eve did. Eve looked at the beautiful fruit. She saw how juicy and sweet it looked, so she took some of it and ate it. Then she gave some of the fruit to Adam, and he ate it too.

That was the saddest day in the world because Adam and Eve disobeyed God. Then they had to be punished.

Satan was happy on that terrible day. He knew that it was the start of sadness and sorrow and pain for everyone. Ever since that day there have been accidents and tornadoes and killing and hurting. People have been hating each other and hating God. This is because Eve and Adam disobeyed God. And all their children disobeyed God. Everyone since that time has been a sinner and has wanted to sin—to do bad things.

People still sin. Even you and I don't always obey God. We do bad things too.

SOME BIBLE VERSES TO READ

Now the serpent was the shrewdest of all the creatures the Lord God had made. "Really?" he asked the woman. "Did God really say you must not eat any of the fruit in the garden?"

"Of course we may eat it," the woman told

him. "It's only the fruit from the tree at the center of the garden that we are not allowed to eat. God says we must not eat it or even touch it, or we will die." *Genesis 3:1-3*

Be careful—watch out for attacks from Satan, your great enemy. He prowls around like a hungry, roaring lion, looking for some victim to tear apart. *1 Peter 5:8*

SOME QUESTIONS TO ANSWER
1. What terrible thing did Eve do?
2. What terrible thing did Adam do?
3. On what day did sickness and death and accidents begin?

SOME THINGS TO PRAY ABOUT
◆ Pray for your pastor and Sunday school teacher.
◆ Thank God for everyone who helps you understand things in the Bible.

God Punishes Sin

IN THE last chapter we read about the terrible thing that happened in the Garden of Eden. Eve listened to Satan and disobeyed God, and so did Adam. Then they had to be punished.

Because the serpent told Adam and Eve to disobey, God let him know that he would be cursed. (That meant God would always be against him.) God said, "You will grovel in the dust as long as you live, crawling along on your belly. From now on, you and the woman will be enemies" (Genesis 3:14-15).

Then God told the woman what it would be

like to give birth to children. This wonderful event would cause her great pain and suffering.

And God said to Adam: "Because you listened to your wife and ate the fruit I told you not to eat, I have placed a curse on the ground. All your life you will struggle to scratch a living from it. It will grow thorns and thistles for you, though you will eat of its grains. All your life you will sweat to produce food, until your dying day. Then you will return to the ground from which you came. For you were made from dust, and to the dust you will return" (Genesis 3:17-19).

As part of their punishment for sin, God made Adam and Eve leave the beautiful Garden of Eden. He put powerful angels and a flaming sword at the entrance of the Garden, so the man and woman could never go back again. Many years later Adam and Eve grew old and died, just as God said would happen because of their sin.

You and I sin too. We sometimes do things God doesn't want us to do. Probably you know that Jesus came to die for your sins. So now God will forgive you if you ask him to. We will read later in this book about Jesus' coming to earth from heaven to take away all of our sins forever. He did this by taking our punishment when he died for our sins.

A BIBLE VERSE TO READ

> Sin makes us die. Through Christ, God gives us life that never ends. *Romans 6:23*

SOME QUESTIONS TO ANSWER

1. What happened to the serpent?
2. What happened to Adam and Eve?
3. What did Jesus do to get rid of your sins?

A PRAYER TO PRAY

> Dear God, I am sorry that I have done bad things. Please forgive me because of what Jesus did for me. Thank you for your kindness in taking away my punishment. In Jesus' name, amen.

PART THREE

JESUS
THE SAVIOR AND KING

God's Wonderful Plan to Save Us

GOD looked down from heaven and saw the terrible thing that happened. He saw Satan talking to Eve. God saw her eat fruit from the tree that he had told her not to eat. Then he saw Adam eat some fruit too.

God's Son, Jesus, also saw what happened, for God the Son was there in heaven. He had always been there with the Father.

Perhaps God the Father said this to Jesus: "Look down on earth. A terrible thing has happened. Adam and Eve have disobeyed us. They listened to Satan and ate the fruit we told them not to eat. Now we must punish them."

We have read in the previous pages of this book that God did punish them. But what about us? You and I have sinned too. We have done things God said not to do. Perhaps you have lied or cheated or stolen something or used bad words. The Bible tells us that the payment for sin is death, but the gift of God is eternal life. What does this mean? It means that God sent Jesus to be punished for your sins. Because God loves you. He does not want to punish his children with eternal death. He wants them to have eternal life. So Jesus agreed to go down to earth and take our punishment. He said that his Father could punish him instead of us. Jesus said he would die in our place.

Think of it! Jesus made the world and stars. He had lived in the glories of heaven forever. Heaven is a wonderful place, where there are thousands of joyful angels and where there is no sickness or sadness or pain or suffering. Yet Jesus, who is greater than all the angels, was willing to leave heaven and come to earth, where there is sin and sickness and sadness. He was willing to come to earth to die for your sins and mine.

Jesus was willing to do all of that because his heavenly Father loved the world so much. God loved all of the people in the world, and he still does. He loves everyone, including you and me.

A BIBLE VERSE TO READ

For God loved the world so much that he gave his only Son so that anyone who believes in him shall not perish but have eternal life.   *John 3:16*

SOME QUESTIONS TO ANSWER
1. What did God see when he looked down on the earth?
2. What did God send Jesus to do?
3. What does the above Bible verse say if you

45

read your name instead of "the world" and "anyone"?

A PRAYER TO PRAY
Thank you, Lord Jesus, for coming from heaven to pay the penalty for my sins. Amen.

An Angel Talks to Mary

WHEN God decided to send his Son, Jesus, to earth, Jesus came as a baby. God chose a teenage Jewish girl named Mary to be Jesus' mother. Mary was engaged to be the wife of a good man named Joseph.

One day Mary was at home. Perhaps she was in the garden. All of a sudden an angel appeared to her! Of course, she was very frightened. She had never seen an angel before. The angel's name was Gabriel. He told her not to be afraid because God had sent him to talk to her. He had some wonderful news. He told her that she was going to have a baby. The baby would be Jesus,

God's Son, who lived in heaven. Jesus was coming down from heaven to earth, and he would be born like anyone else! The angel told Mary that God had chosen her to be the baby's mother.

Mary was too surprised to know what to think.

"How can this be?" she asked the angel. "I've been with no man—there is no one who could be the father of a baby."

Then the angel told her, "God is the baby's father. He will make the baby grow inside you. When the baby is born, you must name him Jesus, for he will be the Savior."

Mary was very happy. *How wonderful,* she thought, *I will be the mother of the Lord Jesus Christ, the Savior of the world! God has blessed me more than any other woman who ever lived.*

What did the angel mean when he said Jesus would be the Savior? He meant that

Jesus was going to come and save people. He would save them from God's punishment for thinking bad thoughts and doing bad things. He would be punished for the sins of Adam and Eve, for your sins and my sins, and for the sins of everyone who believes in him.

A BIBLE VERSE TO READ

"Don't be frightened, Mary," the angel told her, "for God has decided to wonderfully bless you!"   *Luke 1:30*

SOME QUESTIONS TO ANSWER

1. What was the angel's name?
2. What did the angel tell Mary?
3. Are you glad that Jesus came to be the Savior? Why?

A PRAYER TO PRAY

Thank you for sending Jesus down from heaven. Please help missionaries as they tell this Good News to people in other places, such as Africa and Asia and South America. Amen.

Jesus Is Born in a Barn

SEVERAL months after the angel talked to Mary, she and Joseph, who was now Mary's husband, took a trip. They went to the little town of Bethlehem, about fifty miles away. There weren't any automobiles in those days long ago, so they had to walk. Mary probably rode on a donkey.

When they got to Bethlehem, all the rooms for visitors were full. So Mary and Joseph went out to a stable, which was like a barn where the cows and donkeys slept at night.

For nine months the baby Jesus had been growing bigger and bigger inside Mary. On the

night Joseph and Mary arrived in Bethlehem,
Jesus was born! Mary wrapped him up and laid
him on the hay in a manger, which was a box to
hold hay for donkeys and cows.

Do you remember where Jesus was before he was born? Yes, he lived in heaven with God the Father, and with the wonderful Holy Spirit, and with millions of happy angels. Everything in heaven is warm and bright and beautiful, where there is no crying or sadness or sickness or pain or killing or divorce.

Jesus is so great that all the angels fall down and worship him. He is so great that he made all the earth and the stars and the sky. Yet he was willing to leave behind his mighty power and glory and come from heaven to earth to take the punishment for our sins.

Jesus had made the world and could have come to earth as a great king in all his brightness and glory. But then everyone would have been afraid of him. So instead, he was willing to be born as a poor, helpless baby. No one was afraid of a baby!

Jesus grew up and became a man. He was like other people, so no one was afraid of him then either. He could talk to all the people and tell them he loved them. He could tell them about God, and what it was like in heaven, and how to get there.

How thankful we should be that Jesus left his wonderful home in heaven to help us. He came to earth to die on the cross for our sins and to give us everything good.

SOME BIBLE VERSES TO READ

And she [Mary] gave birth to her first child, a son. She wrapped him in a blanket and laid him in a manger, because there was no room for them in the village inn. *Luke 2:7*

He [Jesus] created everything there is— nothing exists that he didn't make. *John 1:3*

SOME QUESTIONS TO ANSWER

1. Why did Jesus choose to come to earth as a baby instead of coming as a great king?
2. What did Jesus leave behind in heaven?
3. Have you asked Jesus to be your Savior? Think about this, and talk to your parents about it.

SOME THINGS TO PRAY ABOUT

◆ Thank Jesus for being willing to come to earth as a baby.
◆ Pray for people who celebrate Christmas but don't know who Jesus is.

Angels Tell the Shepherds about Jesus

ON THE night Jesus was born, some shepherds were out in the fields taking care of their sheep. They were guarding their sheep from wild animals that might hurt them. Suddenly an angel was there among the shepherds! Can you imagine how surprised and frightened they must have been?

The angel told them that their Savior had been born that night in Bethlehem. Then many more angels came and sang, "Glory to God in the highest heaven, and peace on earth for all those pleasing him."

The angels were very excited because God had sent his Son, Jesus, to earth.

When the shepherds heard the news they were excited too. They rushed to the little town of Bethlehem. There they found the stable where the baby Jesus was lying in the manger. The shepherds told Mary and Joseph what the angels had told them about the baby Jesus. Then the shepherds went back to the fields to take care of their sheep. They praised God because they had seen the baby who had come to be their Savior.

We, like the shepherds, are excited about Jesus' coming to be our Savior. You and I must never forget what a wonder this is.

The shepherds are a good example for you to follow:

- ◆ They ran to see the Savior. (You can run to visit with Jesus by praying.)

- ◆ They praised God for sending the Savior, Christ the Lord. (You, too, can praise God and thank him for this wonderful gift.)

- ◆ They told everyone what they had seen and heard about Jesus. (You should do this too. One way you can do this is to ask someone to go along with you to Sunday school next Sunday.)

SOME BIBLE VERSES TO READ

But the angel reassured them. "Don't be afraid!" he said. "I bring you the most joyful news ever announced, and it is for everyone! The Savior—yes, the Messiah, the Lord—has been born tonight in Bethlehem!"

Luke 2:10-11

SOME QUESTIONS TO ANSWER

1. What did the angel tell the shepherds?
2. What were some things that the shepherds did after the angels left?
3. How can you be like the shepherds?

A PRAYER TO PRAY

Dear Father in heaven, I'm excited that you love me. I love you and praise you for being so wonderful. Thank you for sending Jesus to be my Savior. Amen.

Wise Men Bring Gifts to Jesus

WHEN the baby Jesus was about two years old, some men from a faraway country came to visit him. Probably they came on camels and had been traveling slowly for many, many weeks. They were called magi, or wise men. They came because they had seen a special star. It was a very bright star they had never seen before. They knew it was letting them know that a new king had been born. Someday he would be the king over all of God's people.

The wise men traveled toward the star. When they came at last to Bethlehem, they found Jesus. They gave him beautiful presents—the kind of gifts that people give to kings. They got down on their knees in front of the little boy and worshiped him because he was not just an ordinary child. He was going to grow up to be a very special king.

You and I do not need to travel for many weeks before we can worship Jesus. He grew up to be a man, and now he is in heaven. So we can visit him at any time in prayer. He is happy when we come to talk with him and worship him.

Ryan and Cathy were both going to be dressed like the wise men for a Christmas play. Cathy asked Ryan, "Do you know how far the wise men had to travel?"

Ryan said, "I think they traveled about 1,000 miles with their gifts of gold, frankincense, and myrrh."

"Wow!" Cathy said. "I'm glad we don't have so far to go."

"Right," Ryan commented. "We can just close our eyes and visit with Jesus immediately. My dad said that when we thank Jesus, he counts it as a gift. So let's thank him now for coming to earth." And they did.

SOME BIBLE VERSES TO READ
Jesus was born in the town of Bethlehem in Judea, during the reign of King Herod. About

that time some wise men from eastern lands arrived in Jerusalem, asking, "Where is the newborn king of the Jews? We have seen his star as it arose, and we have come to worship him."
Matthew 2:1-2

SOME QUESTIONS TO ANSWER
1. What did the wise men see in the sky?
2. Why did they get down on their knees in front of Jesus and worship him?
3. Where can you go to worship Jesus?

A PRAYER TO PRAY
Thank you, Jesus, that I can come to you and talk with you at any time. Like the wise men, I bring you a gift. My gift to you is my love. I love you with all my heart. Amen.

Jesus Grows to Be a Young Man

JESUS grew up in the village of Nazareth, which was in the land of Israel. Just like other children, he began to walk and talk. Soon he was playing with the other children in the neighborhood. Everybody liked him. Mary's husband, Joseph, was a carpenter, so Jesus probably helped him build things from wood.

When Jesus was a tiny baby, he didn't know he was the Son of God. But by the time he was twelve years old, he understood who he was. At that time Mary and Joseph took him to the temple in the city of Jerusalem. The temple was the building where people went to worship God.

They worshiped God by
praying and giving
offerings to him. They
also worshiped God
by learning about
him.

Jesus began talking
to some important lead-
ers who were there at the temple. He listened to
them and asked them questions. He even gave
them answers to their questions about God.
These educated men were amazed at how much
this twelve-year-old boy knew. Do you know
why Jesus knew so much about God? It is
because God is his Father. Jesus had lived with
God in heaven forever and ever. He had lived
there before he was born! No wonder he could
answer the men's questions!

SOME BIBLE VERSES TO READ

Every year Jesus' parents went to Jerusalem for
the Passover festival. When Jesus was twelve
years old, they attended the festival as usual.
After the celebration was over, they started
home to Nazareth, but Jesus stayed behind in
Jerusalem. His parents didn't miss him at first,

because they assumed he was with friends among the other travelers. But when he didn't show up that evening, they started to look for him among their relatives and friends. When they couldn't find him, they went back to Jerusalem to search for him there. Three days later they finally discovered him. He was in the Temple, sitting among the religious teachers, discussing deep questions with them. And all who heard him were amazed at his understanding and his answers. *Luke 2:41-47*

SOME QUESTIONS TO ANSWER
1. Why did Jesus know so much about God?
2. Where do you go to worship God? Where else can you worship him?
3. What are two ways you can learn about God?

SOME THINGS TO PRAY ABOUT
- Pray for a friend of yours at school.
- Pray for your teacher.

Jesus' Twelve Disciples

"ONE DAY as Jesus was walking along the shore beside the Sea of Galilee, he saw two brothers—Simon, also called Peter, and Andrew—fishing with a net, for they were commercial fishermen. Jesus called out to them, 'Come, be my disciples, and I will show you how to fish for people!' And they left their nets at once and went with him" (Matthew 4:18-20).

Peter and Andrew were the first of twelve men that Jesus chose to be his helpers after he grew up. These twelve men went with Jesus wherever he went. He taught them about God and about heaven, the place where he had lived before he was born.

The twelve men were Jesus' special friends and helpers while he was here on earth. Before he left to go back to heaven, he told them to go everywhere and find other people who would want to be his helpers. He said to invite them to be his followers. And he said to teach the people about him. Anyone who wants to be one of Jesus' disciples can be one.

Jesus wants *you* to be his friend and helper too. He tells you to come to him and follow him. That means you should obey him and help other people learn about him.

Cindy went camping with Megan and her family. The girls sat by the lake catching fish one morning. "This sure is fun," Megan exclaimed as she pulled in another one. "Jesus' disciples were fishermen too. Let's pretend we have a new job—we are his disciples!"

"What do his disciples do?" Cindy asked.

"They believe in him," Megan said. "They go with him and help him. And he teaches them about God."

"That's good," Cindy replied. "How do we apply for the job?"

Megan told her, "Jesus has invited us! We can just tell him yes!"

"I'm going to do it," Cindy said.

Megan added, "I will too."

And because the girls became Jesus' disciples, he helped them as they grew up. He gave them guidance throughout their entire lifetime. He also filled them with love and joy as he showed them how to help others learn about him.

SOME BIBLE VERSES TO READ

Afterward Jesus went up on a mountain and called the ones he wanted to go with him. And they came to him. Then he selected twelve of them to be his regular companions. . . . These are the names of the twelve he chose: Simon (he renamed him Peter), James and John (the sons of Zebedee, but Jesus nicknamed them "Sons of Thunder"), Andrew, Philip, Bartholomew, Matthew, Thomas, James (son of Alphaeus), Thaddaeus, Simon (the Zealot), Judas Iscariot (who later betrayed him).   *Mark 3:13-14, 16-19*

SOME QUESTIONS TO ANSWER

1. Jesus said he would show his disciples how to fish for people. What did he mean?
2. How do you apply to become a friend and disciple of Jesus?

A PRAYER TO PRAY

Lord Jesus, I want to be one of your helpers. Here I am. Please tell me what to do, and I will do it. Amen.

♕
Jesus Has Power to Do Miracles

AFTER Jesus chose his twelve disciples, he began to do wonderful things called miracles. God gave his Son the power to do these things. Here is a drawing of Jesus telling a twelve-year-old girl to come back to life. She had been sick and died. Then Jesus told her to be well. And suddenly she was alive again! How happy her mother and father were!

Jesus did many other great miracles too, such

as feeding over 5,000 people with one small lunch and helping blind people to see. What do Jesus' miracles teach us about him? They teach us that Jesus wasn't just an ordinary person like you or me. He was very special. Jesus' miracles also teach us that he was telling the truth when he claimed to be God's Son. And he was telling the truth when he said he could forgive sins. There was no birth certificate to prove that Jesus was God's Son. And there was no way to prove that a person's sins were forgiven just because Jesus said so. But people could see when Jesus did a miracle. And we can read all about those miracles in the Bible. I'm glad Jesus did miracles to show us who he was, aren't you?

SOME BIBLE VERSES TO READ

> [Jesus told the crowd,] "The child isn't dead. She is only asleep!" They laughed at him, but he told them all to leave. Then he took the little girl's father and mother and his three disciples. And he went into the room where she was lying. Taking her by the hand he said to her, "Get up, little girl!" She was 12 years old. And she jumped up and walked around! Her parents just couldn't get over it. Jesus told

them not to tell anyone about what had happened. Then he told them to give the girl something to eat.   *Mark 5:39-43*

SOME QUESTIONS TO ANSWER
1. What do we call the wonderful things that Jesus could do?
2. What do you think the girl's father and mother said about Jesus after he brought their daughter back to life?
3. Was Jesus an ordinary person? How do you know?

SOME THINGS TO PRAY ABOUT
◆ If you know people who are sick, ask God to take care of them.
◆ Thank God for the strength he gives you each day.

A Widow's Son Comes Back to Life!

ONE DAY Jesus was watching a funeral procession. People were walking down the road carrying a boy's body on some boards. He had died, and they were carrying him to the place where they would bury him. The boy's father was no longer living. So the boy's mother was now alone, with no husband and no son. She and all her friends were crying. Jesus was very sorry for her. When he touched the coffin, the people carrying it stopped walking.

"Don't cry," he told the boy's mother. Then he touched the boy's body. Suddenly the boy was alive again, and he sat up! Everyone was very, very surprised. No one had ever seen a dead boy come back to life again.

Jesus could do wonderful things like that because he is the Son of God. Jesus made the whole wide world, and he can do anything.

When Jesus chose to do this miracle, he showed how much he cared about people. He showed that he had sympathy for the boy's mother. He cared about her and wanted to help her so that she wouldn't be sad. That is a good example for you and me. When someone is sad, we should be sorry for them too. We should ask God to comfort them and to show us how we can help them.

One evening as Alex and his family were talking together, the telephone rang. His father came back with sad news. Mrs. Sanchez, a family friend who lived down the street, had suffered a heart attack that afternoon. The doctors at the hospital hadn't been able to help her, so now she was in heaven, and her husband was all alone. Alex and his family thought of ways to help Mr. Sanchez. Alex had a really good idea. "Let's send him a card and tell him we are praying for him."

"Excellent," said Mother. "And I'll ask him to come over for dinner some evening next week." Father said he would spend time with Mr. Sanchez whenever he could.

Then Alex's little sister, Josie, thought of something the whole family could do for Mr. Sanchez. "Let's go and give him a hug," she said.

So the family prayed for Mr. Sanchez. Then they went to his house to comfort him and hug him. They couldn't bring his wife back to life the way Jesus brought the boy back to life. But they could bring love and comfort to their friend, and that's what they did.

SOME BIBLE VERSES TO READ

Then he walked over to the coffin and touched it. The men who were carrying it stopped. "Young man," he said, "come back to life again." Then the boy sat up and began to talk to those around him! And Jesus gave him back to his mother. *Luke 7:14-15*

SOME QUESTIONS TO ANSWER
1. What did Jesus do for the boy who had died?
2. How could Jesus do such a wonderful miracle?
3. Do you know someone who is sad? How can you can help that person tomorrow?

A PRAYER TO PRAY
Lord Jesus, thank you for making that boy come back to life. I can't do miracles, but I can ask you to help people I know who are sad. Show me what I can do to help too. Amen.

Jesus Tells a Storm to Stop

ONE NIGHT Jesus' disciples were sailing across the Sea of Galilee. They were in their big rowboat with a sail on it. Jesus was sleeping in the back of the boat. A bad storm came up suddenly, and huge waves began coming over the sides of the boat. The waves were filling the boat with water. Soon it would sink, and they would all drown. But Jesus kept on sleeping.

His disciples rushed over to him and shouted, "We're going to sink! We're all going to drown."

Then Jesus woke up. He told the waves to stop coming into the boat. He told the storm to stop and go away. And it did! Suddenly everything was calm and quiet. There weren't any more big waves.

Jesus was disappointed that his friends had been so frightened. They didn't know that Jesus is God, and he can stop storms whenever he wants to. He asked them, "Where is your faith?" He was saying to them, "Why do you think I don't care what happens to you?"

Jesus wants you to expect him to help you. He is in heaven talking to his Father about you, asking him to help you. We must learn to trust Jesus even when it seems like he might be asleep. He isn't!

A BIBLE VERSE TO READ

> The disciples woke him up, shouting, "Master, Master, we're going to drown!" So Jesus rebuked the wind and the raging waves. The storm stopped and all was calm!   *Luke 8:24*

SOME QUESTIONS TO ANSWER
1. What did Jesus tell the storm to do?
2. Why could Jesus do such a wonderful miracle?

3. Can you think of a time when you might feel afraid and need to trust Jesus to help you? Will you expect him to do it?

A PRAYER TO PRAY

Lord Jesus, help me to trust you all the time. Please help me every day when I go to school. Help me to trust you no matter what happens. And show me how to help some other kids when they feel afraid. Amen.

Will Jesus Be the King?

MANY people in Jerusalem were very excited about Jesus' miracles. They wanted him to be their king because he had so much power and could do wonderful things. He did miracles we have read about, such as making a girl and a boy come back to life.

One day Jesus was riding into the city of Jerusalem on a young donkey. Many people went out to meet him on the stony road. They were very happy because they thought Jesus would soon become their king. They threw down their coats on the road in front of him to make a carpet. They were showing their respect for him, just as they would to a king. They took palm branches and walked ahead of him, waving the branches with joy.

The people didn't know that the right time had not yet come for Jesus to be crowned as King. When they were waving the palm branches, the people didn't know that Jesus would die on the cross to take away our sins. That is why he had come from heaven.

Someday Jesus will come from heaven again. Then he will come as our King, with power and great glory. While we wait for him to come back as our King, we can thank him for coming to be our Savior, too. We should let

him know we're sorry when we do things that are wrong. We should also praise him all the time for being both a powerful King and a loving Savior.

SOME BIBLE VERSES TO READ

The next day, the news that Jesus was on the way to Jerusalem swept through the city. A huge crowd of Passover visitors took palm branches and went down the road to meet him. They shouted, "Praise God! Bless the one who comes in the name of the Lord! Hail to the King of Israel!"   *John 12:12-13*

SOME QUESTIONS TO ANSWER

1. What did the people do as Jesus was riding on the donkey?
2. Why did they do this?
3. What can you do for Jesus while you wait for him to come back as your King?

A PRAYER TO PRAY

Lord Jesus, thank you for being my Savior. Please come soon and be my King forever. Amen.

Judas Helps Jesus' Enemies

WE HAVE already read about the great crowd of people waving palm branches and praising Jesus as he rode along on a donkey. They wanted him to be their king. But not everyone wanted this. Jesus' enemies wanted him arrested and killed because he said he was the Son of God and our Savior.

Judas, one of Jesus' disciples, went to these enemies. He may have asked them something like this: "How much will you pay me if I take you to Jesus when no one is around? Then you can arrest him." So they gave Judas a small amount of money, and on Thursday night he

led their soldiers to Jesus. They arrested Jesus and took him away. Then Jesus' disciples ran away and left him. How terrible that Judas betrayed Jesus. And how terrible that his friends all ran away.

The men who arrested Jesus took him to the high priest, who asked Jesus, "Are you the Messiah, God's Son?"

Jesus told him, "Yes, I am."

This made the high priest very angry. He shouted to everyone that Jesus had said a terrible thing because Jesus was just like any other man and was not God's Son. The high priest said Jesus must be killed for saying he was

God's Son. The high priest didn't know that Jesus really is God's Son.

The Roman governor, whose name was Pilate, didn't think Jesus had done anything wrong. But a mob of people yelled to Pilate to have Jesus killed. Pilate was afraid of the mob. So he told his soldiers to let Jesus' enemies kill him.

SOME BIBLE VERSES TO READ

It was now about noon of the day of preparation for the Passover. And Pilate said . . . , "Here is your king!"

"Away with him," they yelled. "Away with him—crucify him!"

"What? Crucify your king?" Pilate asked.

"We have no king but Caesar," the chief priests shouted back.

Then Pilate gave Jesus to them to be crucified.

John 19:14-16

SOME QUESTIONS TO ANSWER

1. Why did the high priest say that Jesus had to die?
2. What could you tell a friend who tries to make you believe that Jesus isn't God's Son?

A PRAYER TO PRAY

Our Father in heaven, thank you for Jesus, my Savior, and his love for me. Help me never to turn against him or pretend not to be his friend, as the disciples did. Amen.

Jesus Dies on a Cross

THIS drawing shows the sad day when Jesus died for our sins. He is the man on the middle cross. The other two men are robbers. The robbers died for their own sins. But Jesus didn't ever sin. That means he didn't have to die. So why did Jesus let people put him on a cross to die? He wanted to do this for us because he loves us. And he knew that God the Father wanted him to do it for you and me, and for everyone. He died so all people can ask him to be their Savior. Then God will forgive their sins.

Do you remember why Jesus left his glorious

home in heaven and came to earth as a baby? He came to grow up and then to die for Adam and Eve's sin, and for your sins and mine. Here in this picture you can see that he did what he came to do. He loved us and wanted to save us by dying for our sins.

Perhaps you have never thought about the fact that you sin. Perhaps you do unkind things, or maybe sometimes you don't obey your parents. Maybe you have told a lie or stolen something. These and many more wrong things are sins for which Jesus died, to erase them from your record book in heaven. He did this for you because he loves you.

You can trust Jesus and believe that he died to save you from your sins. Then God will forgive you, and you won't need to give in to sinful thoughts and actions anymore. God will protect you from being overpowered by the evil in this world and will someday bring you safely home to heaven.

A BIBLE VERSE TO READ

> He died for our sins, just as God our Father planned, in order to rescue us from this evil world in which we live. *Galatians 1:4*

SOME QUESTIONS TO ANSWER
1. Why did Jesus come to earth from heaven?
2. When you believe that Jesus died for your sins, what does God do for you?

SOME THINGS TO PRAY ABOUT
- ◆ Thank Jesus for taking away your sins.
- ◆ Ask Jesus to help you not do things that make God unhappy, but to do things that please him.

God Lets Jesus Die Alone

WHEN Jesus died on the cross, he cried out, "My God, my God, why have you forsaken me?" (Matthew 27:46).

How terrible it was for Jesus when God the Father let him die alone for our sins! Why did God do this to him? It was because God is holy. He is perfect and good and pure and can't allow sin. But when Jesus was on the cross he was filled with our sins. So his Father had to turn away from him. That is why Jesus the Son cried out to God the Father, "Why have you forsaken me?"

Jesus didn't sin, but he carried your sins and my sins and everyone else's sins in his own body. It was as if Jesus had done all of those wrong things himself. So God had to turn away while Jesus died on the cross.

Jesus loves us so much that he was willing to die alone for our sins. Now God can forgive us and bless us and never leave us, for our sins are gone. They can't come between us and God anymore because Jesus took them all and died for them.

If you want Jesus to be your Savior, thank him for dying for your sins.

SOME BIBLE VERSES TO READ
>   [Jesus said,] "I . . . must be lifted up on a pole, so that everyone who believes in me will have eternal life.   *John 3:14-15*
>   Christ died . . . to take away the sins of many people.   *Hebrews 9:28*

SOME QUESTIONS TO ANSWER
>   1. Why did Jesus feel forsaken on the cross?
>   2. What happened to your sins when Jesus died?

SOME THINGS TO PRAY ABOUT
>   ◆ Thank God for never leaving you.
>   ◆ Ask God to help you remember that he is always with you.

◆ Pray for people who don't understand what Jesus did for them on the cross.

The Burial and the Amazing Miracle!

AFTER Jesus died two of his friends came and took his body down from the cross. Then they carried it into a nearby cave and put it there. They rolled a big stone against the opening of the cave. They were very sad as they left his body there. They were sad because Jesus was their hero, and now he was dead. They had thought he was going to be a great king, but instead he had been killed. Now he was dead, and they thought they would never see him again.

But on the third day after Jesus died, the most amazing thing happened! It was early Sunday morning. Some women who were friends of Jesus went out to the cave where his body had been buried. But his body wasn't there! An angel appeared and told the women that Jesus had been brought back to life! The women ran to tell Jesus' disciples the wonderful news.

The disciples didn't believe the women at first. But later that day they were in a room talking about what could have happened to his body. Suddenly Jesus was there with them, talking to them! He didn't open the door, for it was locked. He was just there! Did he come through the walls

or roof? Perhaps he was there all the time, but he hadn't let them see him!

Jesus' friends were scared because they thought he was a ghost. Then Jesus showed them his hands and his feet. He let them see the wounds where he had been nailed to the cross. And he showed them his side, where a soldier had thrust a spear into him while he was on the cross. Then the disciples knew it was really Jesus! They knew that God had raised him to life again after he was dead! How happy and amazed they were! They could hardly believe it.

SOME BIBLE VERSES TO READ

> And just as they were telling about it, Jesus himself was suddenly standing there among them. He said, "Peace be with you." But the whole group was terribly frightened, thinking they were seeing a ghost! "Why are you frightened?" he asked. "Why do you doubt who I am? Look at my hands. Look at my feet. You can see that it's really me. Touch me and make sure that I am not a ghost, because ghosts don't have bodies, as you see that I do!" As he spoke, he held out his

hands for them to see, and he showed them
his feet. *Luke 24:36-40*

SOME QUESTIONS TO ANSWER
1. Where did two of Jesus' friends take his
   body?
2. What did the angel tell the women?
3. Someday you will see Jesus. What do you
   think you will say to him?

SOME THINGS TO PRAY ABOUT
◆ Tell God "thank you" for bringing Jesus
   back to life.
◆ Pray that everyone in your family will know
   that Jesus came back to life.
◆ Pray for your friends.
◆ Pray for people everywhere who don't know
   that Jesus is alive.

Jesus Returns to Heaven

JESUS had come back to life! After that, he appeared to his friends several times during the next few weeks and taught them many things.

One day Jesus took his disciples to a hill called the Mount of Olives near Bethany. While they were there and he was talking to them, suddenly he began rising into the sky! His friends watched in amazement as he disappeared into a cloud! That was the last time they saw him, because he had gone back to heaven. He had gone to be with God his Father.

What a wonderful time that must have been in heaven. Millions of angels may have clapped their hands and cheered because Jesus, their Creator and Lord, had come back home to heaven.

As Jesus' friends stared into the sky and watched Jesus disappear, suddenly two angels were standing beside them. "Why are you looking at the sky?" they asked. "Someday Jesus will return just as you have seen him go!"

Yes, Jesus is coming back again! And when he comes, he will take us with him to our home in heaven. It will be a wonderful place where there is no sorrow or sadness or pain. Perhaps he will come today!

What is Jesus doing now? He is preparing a place for us to live! When it is time for us to live with him, our home will be ready. He is also thinking about you and me, talking to his Father about us and telling him that we are his friends. When we ask God to forgive our sins, Jesus goes to the Father and steps in to plead our case for us. Because Jesus died for us, his Father listens to him and forgives us.

SOME BIBLE VERSES TO READ

Then Jesus led them to Bethany, and lifting his hands to heaven, he blessed them. While he was blessing them, he left them and was taken up to heaven.   *Luke 24:50-51*

SOME QUESTIONS TO ANSWER

1. Where did Jesus go?
2. Will Jesus come back again?
3. What is Jesus doing now?
4. Do you talk to your friends? Is Jesus your friend? Have you talked to him today?

SOME THINGS TO PRAY ABOUT

- ◆ Thank Jesus for being your friend.
- ◆ Ask Jesus to help you tell others that he wants to be their friend too.

Jesus Is Coming Back Again

I WISH Jesus lived here on earth now," Christopher said.

"Why?" his sister asked. "He wouldn't like it down here. There is too much war and fighting and sickness."

"That's why I want him to come back," Christopher said. "He could stop the fighting and make Aunt Melinda get well again and fix everything."

"That would be wonderful," Andrea exclaimed. "I hope he comes today or tomorrow. Do you think he will?"

"I hope so," Christopher said, "but Mrs.

Borden, my Sunday school teacher, read from the Bible that no one knows when he will come. It might be today, but it might be some other time. She said the Bible tells us this will happen:

"There will be a loud trumpet blast in the sky, and Jesus will come in the clouds. Then he will call out to all of his friends, and they will go up to meet him in the air. His friends who have already died will be the first ones to go up. They will meet us there in the sky, and we will always be with Jesus.

"When Jesus comes back, there will be no more cheating or stealing. Even the wild animals will like each other. The foxes won't try to eat the chickens, and the dogs won't chase the cats. Best of all, there won't be wars and soldiers, or even police officers, because they won't be needed. There will be plenty to eat all over the world, and there won't be any divorces or child abuse or any other kind of sin. No wonder the Bible tells us to pray, 'Come back soon, Lord Jesus!'"

Andrea said, "I'm going to pray every day for Jesus to come back soon." Christopher said that he would too. Will you remember to pray also?

SOME BIBLE VERSES TO READ

For in just a little while, the Coming One will come and not delay. *Hebrews 10:37*

In that day the wolf and the lamb will live together; the leopard and the goat will be at peace. Calves and yearlings will be safe among lions, and a little child will lead them all. *Isaiah 11:6*

SOME QUESTIONS TO ANSWER

1. What did Christopher and Andrea decide to pray about every day?
2. Will you try to remember to pray that Jesus will return soon?
3. What will you like best about the time when Jesus comes back?

SOME THINGS TO PRAY ABOUT

◆ Ask Jesus to be your Savior and to forgive your sins so that you will be ready for his return.
◆ Pray that Jesus will come back soon.

PART FOUR

THE
HOLY SPIRIT

The Holy Spirit Comes to the Disciples

FORTY days after Jesus' resurrection he went up into the sky to heaven. Then his disciples went back to Jerusalem to talk and pray together. Ten days later Jesus' friends suddenly heard a roaring sound. It came from the sky above the house where they were staying. It sounded like the noise of a great windstorm, and it filled the house. Then something that looked like a tongue made of fire appeared on the head of each of them. But the fire didn't burn them or hurt them.

Then all of them began talking in languages they hadn't learned! They went outside and talked to people from other countries. Jesus' friends had never learned the languages of those countries. But now they could talk in those languages to tell people about Jesus!

What caused the noise in the sky? Why were Jesus' friends able to speak languages they didn't know? It was because God the Holy Spirit came down upon them and entered into them and stayed within them. The Holy Spirit gave them the power to do miracles! They could heal sick people because God the Holy Spirit was in them.

People today who love Jesus have the Holy Spirit in their life too, just like the disciples did. So can we Christians heal people who are sick? In Africa and other places around the world, missionaries often see wonderful miracles. A missionary might pray for a sick person, who suddenly becomes well again. Sometimes this can happen in our country too. And the Holy Spirit helps every one of us to be kind and good.

How exciting it is to have the Holy Spirit in our heart! He will always help us if we ask him to.

SOME BIBLE VERSES TO READ

On the day of Pentecost, seven weeks after Jesus' resurrection, the believers were meeting together in one place. Suddenly, there was a sound from heaven like the roaring of a mighty windstorm in the skies above them, and it filled the house where they were meeting. Then, what looked like flames or tongues of fire appeared and settled on each of them. And everyone present was filled with the Holy Spirit and began speaking in other languages, as the Holy Spirit gave them this ability.

Acts 2:1-4

SOME QUESTIONS TO ANSWER

1. What caused the noise in the sky?
2. What did the disciples do when the Holy Spirit came into them?
3. Will the Holy Spirit help you be kind and good if you ask him to?

A PRAYER TO PRAY

Dear God, I need the Holy Spirit's help to act the way you want me to. Please make me willing to let him come more and more inside my heart and mind. Then the Holy Spirit will fill me with your love and help me do your work. Amen.

More about the Holy Spirit

WHERE is the Holy Spirit now? He is within you if you have asked Jesus to be your Savior.

What does the Holy Spirit do within us? He gives us joy and patience. He helps us want to do what's right and to be honest all the time. He can even give us love for people we don't like. How glad we can be that Jesus sent the Holy Spirit to us.

We must be careful, though, not to make the Holy Spirit sad. We make him sad if we do things that God doesn't want us to do.

If you disobey God, Jesus won't be happy

either. And God the Father won't be happy.
What a difference it makes in your life if you let
the Holy Spirit help you do what's right.

Barry was always getting mad at his friends. They didn't like this, and Barry didn't like it either. One day after Sunday school, Barry said to his friend, Rick, "I wonder if God would help me get control of my temper if I ask him to?"

Rick told him, "You missed the lesson we had last Sunday on the Holy Spirit of God, so I'll tell you what we learned. The Bible says that when the Holy Spirit comes into our life, he will take away our bad temper and give us peace and patience."

"That's just what I need," Barry said. "How do I get this help from the Holy Spirit? Did you talk about that part too?"

"Yes," Rick told him. "First you ask Jesus to be your Savior. When Jesus comes into your heart, the Holy Spirit does too. He can help you do all the good things that God wants you to do. So you can ask God every morning to help you be patient all day. The Holy Spirit will pray along with you. He will know just what to say to God the Father, who will answer your prayer and help you."

"That's great news, Rick! Thanks for telling me about it," Barry said. "I'm going to talk to God right away and let the Holy Spirit help me."

SOME BIBLE VERSES TO READ

When the Holy Spirit controls our lives, he will produce this kind of fruit in us: love, joy, peace, patience, kindness, goodness, faithfulness, gentleness, and self-control.

Galatians 5:22-23

SOME QUESTIONS TO ANSWER

1. What is Barry going to do to get his temper under control?
2. What other good things will the Holy Spirit help us with? (See today's Bible verses.)

SOME THINGS TO PRAY ABOUT

- ◆ Pray for yourself, that you will always want to do what God wants.
- ◆ Is there something you know God wants you to do, but you don't want to do it? Ask for the Holy Spirit's help to do it anyway.

Good Manners

ONE of the things that pleases God is kindness. One small but important way of being kind is having good manners. If you have good manners at the dinner table, you won't hunch over your food and gulp it down. You won't reach across the table to grab things. You shouldn't act that way when you eat with your family, or when you have guests visiting your home. If you do, they might think you are a sloppy pig! You don't honor God if that is what people think about you.

Another part of good manners is to welcome the guests who come to your house. Jesus would welcome them, and you are his child, so you should welcome them. Stand up and shake hands with them when you are introduced. Don't just grunt and keep on reading or watching TV!

Guests will remember your home as a place where God is honored when you do these simple things to make them feel welcome. Try it and see. Don't be embarrassed by doing right things.

Did you know that the Holy Spirit can help you have good manners? That's because he helps us to be thoughtful and kind. Thoughtfulness and kindness are the basics of good manners.

122

A BIBLE VERSE TO READ

For though your hearts were once full of darkness, now you are full of light from the Lord, and your behavior should show it!

Ephesians 5:8

SOME QUESTIONS TO ANSWER

1. Why is God pleased when you have good manners?
2. Tell about one way that you can improve your manners.

A PRAYER TO PRAY

Dear Father in heaven, I want to behave in ways that bring you honor. Help me to be sensitive to other people's feelings. Help me to respect and honor my parents and other older people. I pray in Jesus' name. Amen.

PART FIVE

THE
CHURCH

Going to Sunday School and Church

ONE afternoon Rosa and Manuel were playing ball in a vacant lot. Manuel and his family had just moved into the neighborhood.

"Rosa, does your family go to church? Can I go with you?" Manuel asked.

"Sure," Rosa said. "Come over at nine o'clock in the morning. We go to Sunday school first and the church service afterwards."

"I haven't been to a church service," Manuel said. "What do you do?"

"Well, we usually sing songs of thanks and praise to God. We also pray to him and ask him to help us obey him all week. We ask him to show us how to be kind to others."

"That sounds awesome," Manuel said. "What else do you do?"

"The pastor tells us what the Bible says about God and his love for us. I don't always understand all of it, but I do get some of it."

"I'd like to know more about God," Manuel said. "I'm glad I can go with you tomorrow. Can I bring my sister too?"

Maybe you have talked to friends about going to church. But did you know that the word *church* has more than one meaning? You might point to your church building and say, "That's my church!" But a church is not just a building. The real church is made up of people. It's made up of all people who believe in Jesus. Usually they meet in church buildings. But they could meet together in a home to sing and pray and learn from the Bible. Or they could meet in a field. Wherever God's people meet, they are part of his church.

A BIBLE VERSE TO READ
> And all the believers met together constantly.
> *Acts 2:44*

SOME QUESTIONS TO ANSWER
1. Can there be a church without a building?
2. How does your church family worship God together? Do you sing? What else?

SOME THINGS TO PRAY ABOUT
- Pray again today for your pastor.
- Ask God to help you think of someone you can invite to Sunday school.

Keeping the Fire Burning

NOW I will tell you why it is very important for you to go to Sunday school and church. It is a time when you and others who love Jesus can help each other. You can talk together with God and worship him with your songs and prayers.

Greta and Erin were camping with their parents. "Will you build a fire, please?" their father asked. So the children got newspapers from the car and one stick of wood. They put the wood on the paper and lit the paper with a match. The paper flamed up around the piece of wood.

"Look at our fire!" Greta shouted. But just

then the flames began to get smaller, and soon they went out. The children were very disappointed.

"Why didn't the wood keep on burning?" Erin asked. Her father explained that a fire needs several pieces of wood. It's hard to keep it burning when there is only one piece.

Now I will ask you an easy question and a hard question.

This is the first question: What happens when you try to start a fire with just one piece of wood? Yes, you are right. And now, the hard question: What happens to Christian boys and

girls who don't go to Sunday school or church? I will tell you. Their love for Jesus often becomes cooler and sometimes finally dies away. But if they spend time at Sunday school and church with others who love Jesus, their love for Jesus becomes stronger.

If you stop going to church, you are like one piece of wood that usually can't burn brightly for God. The Bible tells us that we must keep on meeting together with other Christians. Then the light God gives us can be warm and bright and helpful to others.

A BIBLE VERSE TO READ

And let us not neglect our meeting together, as some people do, but encourage and warn each other, especially now that the day of his coming back again is drawing near. *Hebrews 10:25*

SOME QUESTIONS TO ANSWER

1. Why is it important to have more than one piece of wood when you want to start a fire?
2. Why is it important that you not try to be a Christian all by yourself? What can happen

to your love for Jesus if you don't go to
church or Sunday school?

SOME THINGS TO PRAY ABOUT
- ◆ Thank God for your church family.
- ◆ Ask God to help you go to Sunday school
  and church every week.

Being Baptized

EVEN before Jesus began his wonderful life of healing the sick and raising the dead, his cousin John began baptizing people. John was sent by God to tell people to turn from their sins and turn to God so that they could be forgiven. John baptized people at the Jordan River, which is in the land of Israel. But people can be baptized anywhere after they confess that they have done bad things and God has forgiven them. When people are baptized, they show that they want to live good lives that please God. Even God's Son, Jesus, was baptized. He never did bad things, but he wanted to please God and be a good example for us.

One day the pastor of his church said to Jamie, "I think we should talk to your parents about your being baptized."

"That's what Becky did last Sunday, wasn't it?" Jamie asked.

"Yes," the pastor explained. "Jesus said that his followers should be baptized. Becky is one of his followers, and she wanted everyone to know she is Jesus' friend. So I lowered her into the water in the baptismal tank."

In some churches the pastor submerges the whole person in water, just as the pastor did to Becky. Other pastors dip their hand into a bowl

of water and just touch the head of the person being baptized.*

Perhaps you have already been baptized. If not, you should discuss this with your parents and the pastor. Don't be shy about doing what God wants you to do. Or even if you are shy, be baptized anyway if you belong to Jesus.

A BIBLE VERSE TO READ

People from Jerusalem and from all over Judea traveled out into the wilderness to see and hear John. And when they confessed their sins, he baptized them in the Jordan River.   *Mark 1:5*

SOME QUESTIONS TO ANSWER

1. Have you ever seen someone being baptized? Tell about it.
2. If you haven't been baptized, why should you do that someday?

SOME THINGS TO PRAY ABOUT

◆ Thank God for his Son, Jesus.
◆ Pray for your grandparents.
◆ Pray for your pastor and Sunday school teacher.

*Note to the parent: You can emphasize and further explain whichever type of baptism is used in your church.

Meeting Together for Communion

ONE Sunday morning Brandon and Nicole's father said to them, "Today at our church there will be a Communion service."

Nicole asked, "Don't they sometimes call it the Lord's Supper?"

"Yes, that's right," said Dad. "On the last night before Jesus died, he ate supper with his disciples. He passed around some bread and said, 'This is my body.' Now when Christians break bread into pieces and eat it together, we remember that Jesus' body was broken when he died for us."

"And why are there little cups of juice?" the children asked.

"Jesus passed around a cup of wine," their father told them. "And Jesus said, 'This is my blood. . . . It is poured out to forgive the sins of many.' Today at the Lord's Supper, Christians drink red wine or grape juice. Just like the bread, it's a reminder that Jesus died for us in order to forgive our sins."

"Doesn't our church have the Lord's Supper a lot?" Brandon wanted to know.

"Yes," said Dad. "Jesus wants his followers to eat this special supper often so that we don't forget what he did for us."

"Can we eat it too?" the children asked.

"We will talk to the pastor about it," Father said. "He will help us decide whether you are ready to do this."

SOME BIBLE VERSES TO READ

> As they were eating, Jesus took a loaf of bread and asked God's blessing on it. Then he broke it in pieces and gave it to the disciples, saying, "Take it and eat it, for this is my body." And he took a cup of wine and gave thanks to God for it. He gave it to them and said, "Each of you drink from it, for this is my blood, which seals the covenant between God and his

people. It is poured out to forgive the sins of many."

Matthew 26:26-28

Every time you eat this bread and drink this cup, you are announcing the Lord's death until he comes again.
1 Corinthians 11:26

SOME QUESTIONS TO ANSWER

1. What two things did Jesus pass around to his disciples?
2. When we do this at church, what is the name of this special time?
3. Why do Christians keep on meeting together this way?

SOME THINGS TO PRAY ABOUT

- ◆ Pray that people all over the world will know about Jesus and that he died for them.
- ◆ Pray for two of your friends.

Loving Jesus No Matter What

THE BIBLE tells what happened to Paul and his friend Silas when they were talking to people about Jesus. The two men told how powerful Jesus is, but some of the people who were listening didn't like this. So the city leaders called policemen who took Paul and Silas to jail. There they were whipped with wooden rods until their backs were bruised and bleeding. The man in charge of the jail didn't want them to get away, so he locked their feet between some boards.

Paul and Silas were brave. They prayed all through the night. They even sang songs at midnight! And God sent an earthquake to help set them free.

Thanks to God, we do not have police officers or jailers like that in our country. But in some countries Christians can still be put in jail or killed for telling others about Jesus. However, the Holy Spirit gives them courage and joy. He can help them pray and sing just like Paul and Silas did.

Even in our country we need to stay true to Jesus no matter what. Let me tell you about a girl named Janis. Janis's teacher told her that God didn't make the world—it just happened! Janis got a bad grade on her test because she said only God could make our world, the sun, the moon, and the stars. But Janis didn't care. She wanted to tell the truth about what she believed even if the teacher didn't like it.

SOME BIBLE VERSES TO READ

[The apostle Paul tells what happened to him:]
Three times I was beaten with rods. Once I
was stoned. Three times I was shipwrecked.
Once I spent a whole night and a day adrift at
sea. I have traveled many weary miles. I have
faced danger from flooded rivers and from
robbers. I have faced danger from my own
people, the Jews, as well as from the Gentiles.
I have faced danger in the cities, in the
deserts, and on the stormy seas. And I have
faced danger from men who claim to be
Christians but are not. I have lived with weari-
ness and pain and sleepless nights. Often I
have been hungry and thirsty and have gone
without food. Often I have shivered with cold,
without enough clothing to keep me warm.

2 Corinthians 11:25-27

SOME QUESTIONS TO ANSWER

1. If you knew you would get in trouble for
   talking about Jesus, what would you do?
   Would you stop telling about Jesus? Or
   would you obey God and keep on telling
   about him?

2. How does God help people who get in trouble for talking about Jesus?

SOME THINGS TO PRAY ABOUT
- ◆ Pray for Christians in Muslim countries who are in jail because they love Jesus.
- ◆ Pray that Christians everywhere will show they love Jesus no matter what.

Facing Danger for Loving Jesus

A BOY named Will was reading the morning newspaper and saw a picture from another country. A man and his son were being taken to jail by soldiers because they had been talking to people about Jesus! "That's terrible!" exclaimed Will. "They haven't done anything wrong!"

Will's father said sadly, "There are many countries where people are hurt or killed or put in jail because they are Christians. Sometimes in those countries the government won't allow Christian children to go to school. The government won't let their parents have good jobs, and their families are always hungry. The leaders in those countries don't believe that Jesus is God's Son, the Savior."

"Why don't the Christians tell a policeman about it?" Will asked. "He would make the people stop hurting the Christians."

"No," his father told him, "policemen are told to do it. They won't help."

"Then why doesn't God do something?" Will wanted to know. "He is everywhere, and he sees everything. The Christians should pray and ask God to help them."

"They do," Will's father explained. "Sometimes God sends an angel to rescue them, but usually he doesn't. We don't know why he doesn't always answer their prayers by helping them. But no matter what happens, the Christians love Jesus too much to tell a lie. They would rather die than say they don't love him."

Will thought for a while. Then he looked at the picture again. "I wonder if I will ever have to go to jail for loving Jesus," he said at last.

"Probably not," his father guessed. "But some people may think you are crazy for believing what God tells us in the Bible. And it's no fun to be laughed at. However, that is a small price to pay compared to hurting Jesus by pretending not to love him.

"When it's hard to admit that you're a Christian, you need to ask God for courage."

Will said, "Queen Esther had courage, didn't she? I remember reading a Bible story about her."

"You're right," said Will's father. "God helped Esther to be brave and admit to the king that she was one of God's people. God will help you to be brave too!"

A BIBLE VERSE TO READ
>   Be brave and courageous.   *Psalm 27:14*

SOME QUESTIONS TO ANSWER
>   1. Why were a man and his son taken to jail by soldiers?
>   2. If Christians pray, does God always stop people from hurting them?

SOME THINGS TO PRAY ABOUT
>   ♦ Pray for the Christians who are in danger because they believe in Jesus.
>   ♦ Pray that you will always be loyal to Jesus.

Being Missionaries

WHAT is a missionary?"
Danielle asked her friends Austin and Hannah.

"I know," Austin said. "A missionary is someone who tells people in other countries about
Jesus and what he can do to help them. Some
missionaries are nurses or doctors, and many are
teachers. Some are airplane pilots who take missionaries to places where there aren't any roads."

"Yes," Hannah said. "Our church sends people
to live in Africa to teach people there all about
the Bible."

"That sounds like a good thing to do,"

Danielle replied. "I think I'll be a missionary when I grow up."

"You should pray about it," Hannah told her. "There are millions of kids in other countries who have never heard about Jesus. It will be wonderful if God sends you to tell some of them about Jesus."

Danielle agreed.

Perhaps God will let *you* be a missionary when you grow up. You can pray about this and ask God to tell you what he wants you to do. He will tell you if he wants you to go to other countries or stay right where you are. Wherever you live you can tell the children and their fathers and mothers that Jesus loves them and wants to be their Savior.

Even now you can help Jesus and be like a missionary by inviting your friends to come with you to Sunday school and church.

SOME BIBLE VERSES TO READ

> Therefore, go and make disciples of all the nations, baptizing them in the name of the Father and the Son and the Holy Spirit. Teach these new disciples to obey all the commands

I have given you. And be sure of this: I am
with you always, even to the end of the age.
Matthew 28:19-20

SOME QUESTIONS TO ANSWER
  1. What do missionaries do?
  2. How can you be a missionary now—before
  you grow up?

SOME THINGS TO PRAY ABOUT
  ◆ Pray for a missionary who has been sent by
  your church to a country in Asia, Europe,
  Africa, or South America.
  ◆ Be a missionary now by praying for a friend
  of yours who needs Jesus' help.

PART SIX

GOD & YOU

The Most Important Thing

DO YOU know what the Bible tells us is the most important thing in all the world? Just in case you don't know, I'll tell you. It is to love God. Loving God is the first and greatest commandment. We are to love him with all our heart. We need to love him more and more each day.

Our love for God will grow as we talk to him in prayer and as we get better and better acquainted with him. When we talk with our friends and get better acquainted with them, we learn to love them more. It is the same with God.

Another way to help us love God better is to read about his Son, Jesus, and learn how he helped so many people. As you read the stories in the Bible about Jesus' love and kindness, you will love him and his Father more and more. Then you will be doing the most important thing in the world—you will be loving God.

What is the next most important thing in all the world? The Bible tells us! We should

love other people—our families, our friends, and our neighbors. We must even love our enemies and people who don't like us. This is hard to do, but God will help us if we ask him to.

Abigail and Melanie were neighbors. One day Abigail didn't want to go home at the time her mother had asked her to. "Why aren't you leaving?" Melanie asked her.

"Don't you love your mother?"

"Of course I do!" Abigail replied.

Melanie told her, "You should prove it by doing what she said."

"You're right," Abigail answered. "I love my mother a lot. I'm going to go home now." So Abigail went home, and everyone was happy about it. So was God, who was watching and listening. I think he smiled!

God wants you to love him and to be his best friend. That is why he made you. He also wants you to love other people. That's because he made them and loves them, too!

SOME BIBLE VERSES TO READ

> Jesus replied, "'You must love the Lord your God with all your heart, all your soul, and all your mind.' This is the first and greatest commandment. A second is equally important: 'Love your neighbor as yourself.' All the other commandments and all the demands of the prophets are based on these two commandments."   *Matthew 22:37-40*

SOME QUESTIONS TO ANSWER

> 1. What are the two most important things in all the world?

2. What are some ways that you can show God that you love him?
3. What are some ways that you can show other people that you love them?

A PRAYER TO PRAY

Father in heaven, how glad I am that you love me. I love you, and I want to love you more and more. I want to always love and obey you. Help me to do this. Amen.

God Knows Everything

"I LEARNED a lot in school today," Keri told her mother.

"I'm glad," her mother said. "You have learned a lot this year. But do you know someone who knows more than you do?"

"My teacher," Keri said. "She's real smart."

"Yes," Mother said, "but I'm thinking of someone who knows even more. He knows everything."

"Oh," Keri said, "I think you're talking about God."

"Right!" Mother told her. "God knows what you did at school today, and he knows what you did yesterday. He loves you and knows your name and where you live. He knows what everyone in the world is doing. He knows everything! He knows what you want for your birthday, but he also knows what is best for you and what isn't. He sees when you are helping, and that makes him glad. He sees when you pout or do things that are wrong, and that makes him sad."

Yes, God knows everything. He knows what is best for you, and he will tell you what to do if you ask him. Should you be a car mechanic or a dentist when you grow up? Or which of a hundred other kinds of jobs should you have? Or should you be an overseas missionary and go to another country to tell people there that Jesus is the Savior?

How good it is that God will help you know what is best. It would be foolish not to ask him and not to get his help and his wisdom.

SOME BIBLE VERSES TO READ

I am God, and there is no one else like me. Only I can tell you what is going to happen even before it happens. *Isaiah 46:9-10*

SOME QUESTIONS TO ANSWER

1. Do you know what you will probably do next week? Talk about some of these things.
2. Who knows what you will do next year?
3. Why can God help you make good decisions?

A PRAYER TO PRAY

Lord God, thank you that I can talk to you like this, and that you are listening as I pray. I am glad that you know all about me and that you know what is best for me to do. Please be my guide all the time, for all my life. Amen.

God Is Everywhere at the Same Time!

WHERE'S Alan?" his brother Shawn asked. "I thought he was upstairs, but I can't find him. I want him to play with me."

"He went over to Jason's house," Mother said.

"You always know where we are," Shawn said.

"Not always," she replied. "But God always knows because he is always with both of you."

"He is?" Shawn asked in surprise. "I thought God was up in heaven."

"Yes," Mother said. "He is. And he is here in the room with us now. He is also with your father at work. He is even with Uncle Jim far away in Japan. God is everywhere."

"Does he go to all these places every day?" Shawn asked.

"He stays everywhere all the time," Mother explained. "He is always with you wherever you go. He is always with Alan all the time. And he is always everywhere else at the same time!"

Shawn's mother was telling him about something that's not easy to figure out. We cannot begin to understand how someone could be two places at the same time. Yet the Bible tells us that God is everywhere at once! We know this from the Bible, and we know it from our own experience. In the story Shawn and Alan were at two different houses, but God was with each of them, and each of them could talk to him. Uncle

Jim, who was thousands of miles away in the country of Japan, could talk to God because God was there with him. And God was at the office with the boys' father, helping him there.

How wonderful God is—far too great for us to understand. And yet he is a loving Father who wants you to be in his family. You *are* part of God's family if you have asked Jesus to forgive your sins and to be your Savior.

SOME BIBLE VERSES TO READ

> If I go up to heaven, you are there; if I go down to the place of the dead, you are there.
>
> *Psalm 139:8*

> The Lord is watching everywhere, keeping his eye on both the evil and the good.
>
> *Proverbs 15:3*

> "Can anyone hide from me? Am I not every-where in all the heavens and earth?" asks the Lord.
>
> *Jeremiah 23:24*

SOME QUESTIONS TO ANSWER

1. Is God with us now, here in this room?
2. Is he in heaven now too?
3. Name some other places where he is right now.
4. Is he in your heart?

SOME THINGS TO PRAY ABOUT

- ◆ Thank God for loving you and never leaving you.
- ◆ Pray for your teacher at school, and pray for the principal.

There Is Only One God

THERE is only one God. Some people in countries such as India think there are many gods, but that isn't true. Some people in Africa say a tree or a rock or a mountain is their god! But they are wrong. A tree is not God. It can't even think! Our God is the only God there is. He made the heavens and the earth, the stars, and all the plants and animals and birds.

Pastor Smith was visiting the children in Sunday school. It was the third-grade class. He talked to the children about God. He asked them, "How many gods are there?"

All the kids told him, "There is only one God."

"That is right," the pastor said. Then he told them, "Put on your thinking caps!" He was telling them to think hard about what he was going to say. Then he told them, "Our Father in heaven is God, and Jesus is God, and the Holy Spirit is God!"

A boy named Jason asked the pastor, "Are there three Gods?"

"No," the pastor said. "There is only one God. God the Father, God the Son, and God the Holy Spirit are all parts of each other. Together they are only one God."

Then he told the class, "Please repeat these words: Our heavenly Father is God."

So the class repeated the words.

Then the pastor said, "Jesus is God," and the class repeated, "Jesus is God."

And then the pastor said, "The Holy Spirit is God."

And the class repeated, "The Holy Spirit is God."

Finally, he said, "And these three are one God."

The class said, "And these three are one God."

That is the end of the story about Pastor Smith, but now I want you to say aloud what the class said:

- ◆ "Our heavenly Father is God.
- ◆ Jesus is God.
- ◆ The Holy Spirit is God.
- ◆ And these three are one God."

In the previous devotional we read that God is everywhere at once, and now we have learned another truth about God. It is very hard to understand, but it is very important to know: *There is only one God.*

A BIBLE VERSE TO READ

And there is only one God and Father, who is over us all and in us all and living through us all. *Ephesians 4:6*

SOME QUESTIONS TO ANSWER

1. If someone asks you how many Gods there are, what will your answer be?

2. If a Muslim tells you that Christians believe in three gods, what will you say?

A PRAYER TO PRAY

Thank you, God, for telling us that there is no other God but you. Help me to love and trust and obey you. Amen.

How to Get to Heaven

IF I'M good enough, will I get to heaven?" That is the question a boy named Jon asked his Sunday school teacher.

The teacher asked, "Do you think anyone could ever be good enough to get to heaven?"

Jon thought for a while and then said, "Well, I'm almost good enough. I've never killed anybody."

"Have you ever told a lie?" the teacher asked.

"Well, yes, once I did when I said I hadn't taken some cookies."

"You stole the cookies?" the teacher asked. "And then lied about it? That's two bad things—two sins. There can't be even one sin in heaven."

Jon looked sad. "I don't think I'll ever get to heaven. I've already done too many wrong things."

"Not so fast," his teacher told him. "Everyone in the world has sinned. No one anywhere is good enough. But haven't you forgotten something?"

What do you think Jon forgot? The teacher told him, "Somebody who *is* good enough came to earth from heaven. He died to take away your sins."

Jon's face brightened. "Yes!" he exclaimed, "God sent his Son, Jesus, to be punished for my sins. So I can go to heaven someday even though I'll never be good enough!"

"That's right," the teacher said. "I know you have asked God to forgive your sins. So he doesn't even remember the bad things you've done."

During prayer time Jon said to God, "Thank you, thank you for forgiving me. Thank you that I can go to be with you in heaven when I die."

SOME BIBLE VERSES TO READ

Listen! In this man Jesus there is forgiveness for your sins. Everyone who believes in him is freed from all guilt and declared right with God.
Acts 13:38-39

SOME QUESTIONS TO ANSWER

1. Have you ever done any wrong things? Do you remember what you did?
2. Will God forgive you if you ask him to? Will he remember the bad things you've done?

SOME THINGS TO PRAY ABOUT

- ◆ Thank Jesus for dying to take away your sins.
- ◆ Ask God to forgive you for the bad things you've done.
- ◆ Tell God how happy you are that you can go to be with him in heaven someday.

What If I Sin Again?

IN THE last story we read about a boy named Jon who learned that he can go to heaven even though he will never be good enough. But the next Sunday when the teacher saw him, he was sad again. "What's the matter?" the teacher asked.

"I can't go to heaven after all," he said sadly.

"Why not?" the teacher wanted to know.

Jon explained that he had done something wrong the day before, so Jesus wouldn't want him now. The teacher reminded him, "You told me last week about two wrong things you did. Did Jesus come all the way from heaven to die for only the two sins? No, he died for *all* your sins. Maybe you will do something wrong this week too, but Jesus has died for that sin too. Tell Jesus what you did, and ask him to forgive that sin too. Then try never to do it again."

Now Jon was smiling once more. "That's really great," he said. "Is that what I should do every time I do something wrong? Tell Jesus I'm sorry? And ask him to forgive me?"

"Exactly," his teacher said.

Then Jon had another question. "Can I just be bad as much as I want to? Will Jesus still forgive me?"

"No," the teacher explained. "If you don't care how much bad you do, it is because you're not letting Jesus have the most important place in your heart. And you aren't letting the Holy Spirit control your actions. You may not even be one of God's children."

"But I love Jesus. And I do care about the bad things I do," Jon said.

The teacher told him, "I know you do. Whenever you are sorry, ask God to forgive you. He will forgive you because of what Jesus did for you."

A BIBLE VERSE TO READ

If we confess our sins to him, he is faithful and just to forgive us and to cleanse us from every wrong.

1 John 1:9

SOME QUESTIONS TO ANSWER

1. Can people go to heaven even if they sometimes do things that are bad?
2. How is this possible?

SOME THINGS TO PRAY ABOUT

- ◆ Thank God for helping you do what's right.
- ◆ Tell God you're sorry about the times when you didn't let him help you.
- ◆ Pray for a missionary you know.
- ◆ Name someone you are thankful for, and thank God for that person.

You Can Live Forever with Jesus

IN TODAY'S newspaper you can probably find a story about someone who did something bad. Maybe a man robbed a bank, or perhaps he killed someone. Now he is in jail so that he can't hurt anyone else. Probably he will be sent away to a large prison, where he will live the rest of his life.

That illustrates what will happen to Satan someday. When we go to live in heaven, do you know where Satan and his evil angels will be? God has prepared a place of terrible sadness for them, far away from God and far away from heaven. Satan will live there forever.

Then he will never be able to hurt us or bother us again.

People who refuse to love God will, just like Satan, be unable to live with God. That is why you and I must always try to help our friends and other people know that Jesus wants them to be with him in heaven. He doesn't want anyone to have to be with Satan. Instead, people can belong to Jesus and live with him in heaven forever. They won't have to be in darkness and sadness forever.

When Jesus comes back, there will be a great Judgment Day. God's record books will be opened, with everyone's name inside. In which book will your name be written? If you have asked Jesus to be your Lord and Savior, your name will be in the Book of Life. It might say something like this: "_____ is God's child. Bring this person to heaven." And there will be a reward for all the good things you have done.

SOME BIBLE VERSES TO READ

The Lord . . . does not want anyone to perish.
2 Peter 3:9

And I saw a great white throne, and I saw the one who was sitting on it. The earth and sky fled from his presence, but they found no place to hide. I saw the dead, both great and small, standing before God's throne. And the books were opened, including the Book of Life. And the dead were judged according to the things written in the books, according to what they had done.   *Revelation 20:11-12*

SOME QUESTIONS TO ANSWER
   1. Where does God want you to live forever?
   2. Who has saved you from having to go live far away from God?

SOME THINGS TO PRAY ABOUT
   ◆ Thank God for heaven.
   ◆ Pray for people who need to know that they can live forever with Jesus.

When to Say, "I'm Out of Here"

A GIRL named Brittany learned about Jesus at Sunday school. She found out that Jesus had died for her sins.

"Thank you, Father in heaven," she prayed. "Thank you for sending Jesus to die for me. Thank you for taking away my sins. Help me to do what is right. If other kids are doing something bad, help me to walk away. Help me to leave, even if they call me names for not doing what they want me to do."

One day some other kids wanted Brittany to go with them and do something bad. But Brittany told them, "No, I don't do things like that. They are wrong. Good-bye!" And she walked away. The others laughed at her. But Brittany wouldn't come back until they quit doing what was wrong. The

Holy Spirit was inside Brittany, helping her refuse to do wrong.

There may be times when you must decide whether to follow friends who are doing wrong or to do the right thing. God will help you say no and walk away. You can say, "Absolutely not. I'm out of here!" Let's hear you say it.

A BIBLE VERSE TO READ
 Turn away from evil and do good. *1 Peter 3:11*

SOME QUESTIONS TO ANSWER
 1. Why did Brittany sometimes walk away from the other kids?
 2. What might other children say to you if you walk away from them when they are doing something wrong?

SOME THINGS TO PRAY ABOUT
 ◆ Ask God to give you courage so you'll refuse to do what is wrong, even if other kids want you to do something bad.
 ◆ Ask God to help you think of something good to do in place of something bad.

Discipline Is Good for You!

THERE was a man who never disciplined his two children, Greg and Kathy. They could do anything they wanted to. He never told them, "Don't do that!" So they didn't learn how important it was to obey their parents and teachers. They misbehaved all the time.

One day after school all the neighborhood kids were playing soccer. They let Greg and Kathy play, but Kathy didn't want to follow the rules, and Greg made fun of everyone who missed a kick. Both Kathy and her brother did other wrong things like that. After a while nobody wanted to play with them or go bicycling with them or have

them on their soccer teams. So Greg and Kathy had to miss out on lots of fun, all because their father never stopped them from being selfish and rude.

The children's father had a vegetable garden where he raised carrots, tomatoes, peas, and beans. He didn't allow any weeds in his garden. He got rid of them all. A friend asked him a dumb question: "Why do you take out the weeds?"

"They grow faster than my tomato plants," the children's father replied. "The weeds choke out the good plants, so they can't grow."

"It's the same with your children," his friend said. "The things they do wrong will choke out the good things you have planted in their life. Don't spoil their life by never telling them no!"

SOME BIBLE VERSES TO READ

If you refuse to discipline your children, it proves you don't love them; if you love your children, you will be prompt to discipline them.
Proverbs 13:24

Teach your children to choose the right path, and when they are older, they will remain upon it.
Proverbs 22:6

SOME QUESTIONS TO ANSWER

1. What does the Bible tell your parents to do when you do wrong things?
2. When you do wrong, how does punishment help you?
3. What bad things can happen to you if your parents don't discipline you?

SOME THINGS TO PRAY ABOUT

- ◆ Thank God for your parents and for the ways they show their love for you.
- ◆ Pray that you will learn to happily obey your parents.

More about Discipline

KRISTIN, her twin sister Karin, and their cousin Melinda were all in kindergarten. One day when their families were vacationing together, the girls were walking to the beach. They were talking about their mothers.

"Is your mother a mean mother?" the twins asked Melinda.

Melinda said, "No! My mother isn't mean!"

"But we think she is," Kristin and Karin said. "You said she spanked you when you told her a lie."

"Sure she did," Melinda said, "but that's what she's supposed to do. She kissed me afterwards

and said if she let me tell lies, I'd grow up to be a liar. I don't want to be like that. I know a boy you can never believe because he's such a liar. His parents should scold him. I'm glad my parents don't let me tell lies or do other bad things."

Yes, Melinda is right. Children who aren't punished for the bad things they do will lose respect for their parents and teachers. They may think they can do whatever they like, so they'll get into all sorts of trouble. Worst of all, they might think that since parents' rules can be broken without punishment, then God's rules can be broken too. Their entire life can be messed up because their parents don't punish them when they do things that are wrong.

So whether you are big or little, please understand that your parents must discipline you for doing things that are wrong. Perhaps they will need to spank you or ground you. Be thankful that they are helping you learn to obey. And remember that children learn to obey God by obeying their parents.

A BIBLE VERSE TO READ

Scolding and spanking a child helps him to learn. Left to himself, he brings shame to his mother.   *Proverbs 29:15*

SOME QUESTIONS TO ANSWER

1. What are some good ways for mothers and fathers to teach their children to do what's right?
2. What are some reasons your parents may need to scold you?

SOME THINGS TO PRAY ABOUT

◆ Pray that you will want to do things that make your parents proud of you.
◆ Ask God to help you learn to obey him as you learn to obey your parents.

❧ Obeying Your Parents

MAX is a boy in second grade. He was playing with his friends in his yard. Just that morning his mother had said to him, "Remember our rules. You must never go anywhere without telling me where you are going."

"OK," Max had said.

But now Eric, one of the older boys who was playing with Max, had an idea that sounded like fun. He said, "Let's go down to the store and buy some candy."

"I have to tell Mom first," Max said.

"Don't be silly," Eric told him. "She'll never know. We'll be back in a few minutes."

"But I shouldn't go without telling her," Max said. "It's one of the rules at my house."

The other children called Max a scaredy-cat and a mama's boy. They said they would go without him and wouldn't be his friends anymore. So Max went with them. He got back before his mother even knew he had left. But God saw what Max did. God knew that he had disobeyed.

Max did wrong because his friends talked

him into it. What would you do if your friends told you to do something your parents had told you not to do? I hope you would tell them to go away. Your parents know what is best for you. And even more important than that, you are obeying God when you obey your parents.

A BIBLE VERSE TO READ

But remember that the temptations that come into your life are no different from what others experience. And God is faithful. He will keep the temptation from becoming so strong that you can't stand up against it. When you are tempted, he will show you a way out so that you will not give in to it.   *1 Corinthians 10:13*

SOME QUESTIONS TO ANSWER

1. Why did Max disobey?
2. What are some of the rules at your house?
3. What can you do when someone tries to get you to disobey?

SOME THINGS TO PRAY ABOUT

- ◆ Thank God for your parents, and pray for them.
- ◆ Tell God you're sorry if there are times when you have not obeyed your parents.

Conscience Is a Hard but Very Important Word

THERE is a little voice inside you that lets you know when you are doing something that's wrong. It's called your conscience. This voice doesn't talk out loud and tell you, "Stop doing that!" But you can hear it in your mind. It is one of God's ways of talking to you.

Another voice in your mind may tell you to go ahead and do the wrong thing. That is Satan talking to you.

How can you tell which voice to obey? Your

conscience will help you know what pleases God. Those are the things you should do.

God teaches your conscience what to tell you. One of the ways he does this is by helping your conscience recall what you read in the Bible. That is a good reason to read some of God's instructions in the Bible every day.

Do you know what happens if you don't listen to your conscience? What if you keep on doing something it tells you not to do? After a while it quits talking to you. Why should it waste its time with you if you won't listen? The little voice gets weaker and weaker, until finally you've lost your conscience, one of the best friends God gave to help you. So now you are alone, without the help you need to be safe from Satan. You won't be able to fight Satan by your-self. You will lose. You need Jesus to help you. So ask God to give your conscience back to you again. When it tells you don't, then *don't*.

A BIBLE VERSE TO READ

Always keep your conscience clear, doing what you know is right. For some people have disobeyed their consciences and have deliber-ately done what they knew was wrong. It isn't

surprising that soon they lost their faith in
Christ.   *1 Timothy 1:19*

SOME QUESTIONS TO ANSWER
1. What is a name for the little voice inside
   you that tells you what is wrong for you
   to do?
2. What happens if you don't listen?

SOME THINGS TO PRAY ABOUT
- Thank God for giving you a conscience.
- Ask God to help you always obey him and
  not listen to Satan.

Reading the Bible

I READ some verses or stories from the Bible every day," Dave told Lindsay.

"That sounds like a good idea," she said. "I guess I'll try doing that too. What is it about?"

"It's awesome! It tells about Jesus walking on the water and making sick people well and helping dead people to be alive again," Dave said. "Sometimes my pastor reads God's rules from it. We need his rules to keep us from doing wrong things and wrecking our life."

"But my teacher at school doesn't think so," Lindsay said. "He says there isn't any God to make rules, so we can do whatever we want to. He says nothing is bad and everything is good."

"That's crazy," Dave said. "If nothing is wrong, then everybody would be stealing and cheating. There have to be laws, and who can make better laws than God? He knows everything. He made us, and he knows what is best for us."

"Does your teacher know you read the Bible every day?" Lindsay wanted to know.

"Yes. One time he told the class that there isn't any God. He asked if anybody could prove there is, so I told him what Psalm 19:1 says: 'The heavens tell of the glory of God.' But my teacher said that the stars just happened. They don't

prove anything about God. He said to quit reading the Bible, or I'd become weird! Well, now I've memorized some other verses for him if he ever asks me again!"

Yes, we should read some of the Bible every day. It is God's letter to us, and it tells about his good plans for us. If you haven't been reading the Bible regularly, or perhaps not at all, why not begin today? It will do you a world of good and will help you know more about our Lord Jesus Christ. Get your Bible now. Find the book written by Mark, and begin reading there.

A BIBLE VERSE TO READ
> The heavens tell of the glory of God. The skies display his marvelous craftsmanship. *Psalm 19:1*

SOME QUESTIONS TO ANSWER
1. Read the Bible verse again. How do the heavens talk?
2. True or false: It is a good idea to read a Bible story or other parts of the Bible every day.
3. When do you read your Bible? (If you haven't been reading your Bible, when would be a good time each day to do this?)

4. Do you have some favorite verses? Do you have a favorite Bible story?

A PRAYER TO PRAY

Dear Father in heaven, help me to understand what I read about you in the Bible. Teach me about your power and glory. Thank you for making the sun and moon and all the stars. And thank you for making me. Amen.

Talking to God about Everything

GOD likes us to talk to him. He is never too busy to listen to his children. Perhaps you pray to him before you eat, thanking him for the food. Perhaps you pray at bedtime or family devotions, too. Maybe you thank God for helping your parents have enough money to buy food at the grocery store. Perhaps you talk to God about the things that have happened during the day. You might tell him what you did at school or while you were playing. God is interested in everything you do. It pleases him when you talk things over with him. He knows all that happened without your telling him, but he likes to have you share your thoughts with him.

You can pray anytime, wherever you are. You can say "Thank you" and "Please help me." You can ask God for anything. Some of the things you ask for may not be good for you, so he answers your prayer by saying no. But he is glad to give you many of the good things you ask for. Often he is just waiting for you to ask.

Sometimes you will want to ask God to help missionaries in faraway places. You will want to pray for your family and for the people who live around you and for the leaders of our country. Pray for government leaders, such as the president, the justices of the Supreme Court, the senators, the members of Congress, and the governor of your state. God tells us to pray for all of these people, so we should not forget to do this.

God is pleased when we pray, so let's please him.

SOME BIBLE VERSES TO READ

Pray all the time. Ask God for anything in line with the Holy Spirit's wishes. Plead with him, reminding him of your needs, and keep praying earnestly for all Christians everywhere.

Ephesians 6:18

Pray . . . for kings and all others who are in authority over us. *1 Timothy 2:2*

SOME QUESTIONS TO ANSWER

1. When are good times to pray every day?
2. What are some good things to ask God for?

SOME THINGS TO PRAY ABOUT

- ◆ Pray for a local government leader and for a national leader.
- ◆ Pray for a missionary.
- ◆ Thank God for your family and friends.
- ◆ Tell God all about your day.

Thanking God

JEREMY and Kyle were talking about prayer. "It's so awesome to be able to talk to God," Jeremy said.

"Right," Kyle replied. "Just think, we can talk to the God who created billions of stars! And he listens to us!"

"It's amazing," Jeremy said. "What do you talk to God about when you pray?"

"Well, first I thank him for all the good things he gives us."

"You mean, like our parents and homes?" asked Jeremy. "I do that too. And I praise God because he is so great and good. Of course, I also ask him for lots of things."

The kids talked for quite a while about God, and then they talked about when to pray.

"My family prays before we eat," Kyle said. "And we pray when we're at church or Sunday school."

"We do too," Jeremy said. "Also, I pray before I go to bed, and sometimes when I wake up."

The boys were right in what they said about prayer.

Praying isn't just asking God to give us things. That is only part of it. Another part of prayer is praising him for the awesome God that he is. Still another part is thanking God for all the good things he gives to us. He gives us mothers and fathers to love us. He may give us a brother or sister or friends. He also helps us to have warm houses and good things to eat. So thank God for these good things.

SOME BIBLE VERSES TO READ
>It is good to give thanks to the Lord, to sing praises to the Most High. It is good to proclaim your unfailing love in the morning, your faithfulness in the evening. *Psalm 92:1-2*

Pray about everything. Tell God what you need, and thank him for all he has done.

Philippians 4:6

SOME QUESTIONS TO ANSWER
1. What are some of the good things God has given you?
2. How can you show God that you are thankful for these good things?

SOME THINGS TO PRAY ABOUT
- Today, instead of asking God for anything, tell him you love him, and praise him because he is so great and good.
- Think about what God has done for you in the last week, and thank him.

Giving Your Money Back to God

TIMOTHY and Chris were talking about what to do with the money they earned on their paper routes. "I'm saving up to buy a telescope," Timothy said. Chris said he wanted to have a better bicycle.

"That will be neat," Timothy agreed. "But there's something else we should do with part of our money."

"What's that?" Chris asked.

Timothy told him, "God helps us earn our money, so it all really belongs to him. The Bible says everything we have comes from God. So we should give some of it back to him. I want to give some money to the Salvation Army to help poor people who need food."

"That's good," Chris said. "Maybe I'll give some to our church's mission fund. I want to help send missionaries to other countries so they can tell people there about Jesus."

"How much should we give?" Timothy wondered.

Chris replied, "Mr. Jefferson, my Sunday school teacher, said he gives 10 percent of his salary for God's work. Each time I earn a dollar, if I give 10 percent, that would be ten cents I could give. I'm going to do it!"

"So will I," Timothy agreed.

I am glad that Chris and Timothy will give away some of their money to others. God wants us to do this. He loves a cheerful giver, and he will care for all their needs.

A BIBLE VERSE TO READ

Godly people give generously to the poor.
Their good deeds will never be forgotten.

2 Corinthians 9:9

SOME QUESTIONS TO ANSWER

1. Should you give part of your money to
   God?
2. Who is happy when you give?
3. The next time you get some money, what
   might you do with it?

A PRAYER TO PRAY

Lord, thank you for telling me in the Bible that
you want me to help people who are poor
and hungry. Please make me very happy to
give away some of the money you help me to
have. Amen.

Living as Jesus Wants You To

ROBERTO thought and thought. His mother had asked him a question, and he was thinking about the answer. His mother had asked him, "How do boys and girls who love Jesus act differently from those who don't love him?"

Roberto finally replied, "Well, for one thing, we don't tell lies or cheat or steal stuff. And we do what our parents tell us."

"Yes," mother said. "Those are all good things. Anything else?"

"Another thing is that we don't laugh or make fun of anyone, like some kids do," Roberto said.

Mother replied, "Yes, it is important to please God by the things we do. But it is just as important to please him by the things we say. What do you do if other children say things that are unkind or tell jokes that are not nice?"

"I know what we *should* do, but we don't always do it," Roberto said. "We should walk away and not play with them until they quit talking that way."

Mother told him, "That's right. You can ask God to help you say and do what's right and run away from what is wrong."

"OK," Roberto said, "That's what I'll do."

One day a neighbor saw Roberto in his yard and stopped to talk to him. "Roberto," he said, "I like the way you act and the way you talk. You are polite to grown-ups and kind to your friends. Everyone can count on you to tell the truth and do what's right. Not all the kids around here are like that. Tell me something. Do you love Jesus?"

"I sure do!" Roberto told him.

And the neighbor said, "I thought so."

A BIBLE VERSE TO READ

May the words of my mouth and the thoughts of my heart be pleasing to you, O Lord, my rock and my redeemer.   *Psalm 19:14*

SOME QUESTIONS TO ANSWER

1. Why is it important to say things that are kind and true?
2. How do you act differently from the way some kids act?

SOME THINGS TO PRAY ABOUT

◆ Pray for someone that others often make fun of, and ask God to show you how to be kind to that person.
◆ Ask God to help you say and do what's right at school tomorrow and all the time.

The Throne in Your Heart

A KING sits on a beautiful chair called a throne. From there he tells the people in his country what to do.

Do you know that you have a throne in your heart and that someone is sitting on it to tell you what to do? It's not a real chair, of course. But there is a real king who tells you what to do. That king should be the Lord Jesus. He is the one who has the right to be on the throne of your life. He made you and then died for you. So he is the only one who should sit on the throne in your heart.

But there are two other people who want to sit on the throne and tell you what to do. One of them is Satan. He wants to sit there and tell you to do bad things. But you can tell him, "Get out of here, Satan! Only Jesus can sit on the throne of my life." When you tell Satan that, he goes away. God gives you power over Satan.

There is a third person who wants to sit on the throne and tell you what to do. The third person is you! If you are on the throne, Satan is happy. He knows he can get you to be selfish and to do many bad things. So it is wrong for you or Satan to be in charge of your life. It is only Jesus who has that right.

Invite Jesus now to sit on the throne in your heart and to be in charge of your life. He will gladly do many good things for you if you will let him. And he will keep you from making a mess of your life.

SOME BIBLE VERSES TO READ
Next the Devil took [Jesus] to the peak of a very high mountain and showed him the

nations of the world and all their glory. "I will give it all to you," he said, "if you will only kneel down and worship me."

"Get out of here, Satan," Jesus told him. "For the Scriptures say, 'You must worship the Lord your God; serve only him.'"   *Matthew 4:8-10*

SOME QUESTIONS TO ANSWER
1. Who are the three people who want to sit on the throne in your heart and tell you what to do?
2. Have you invited Jesus to sit on the throne in your heart? If you haven't, why not do it now?

SOME THINGS TO PRAY ABOUT
- Ask God to help you keep his Son, Jesus, on the throne in your heart.
- Thank God for the good things his Son has done for you—and will keep on doing if you let him be in charge.

♥
Giving Glory to God

ISN'T this a beautiful day?" Jennifer remarked to her brother Jim. "The sun is shining, the birds are singing, the flowers are blooming. Do you think God likes days like this too?"

"I don't know about that," Jim told her, "but I know he likes it when we are happy."

"Did God put us here on earth so we'd be happy?" Jennifer wondered.

"He wants us to be happy, but that's not why he put us here," Jim told her. "At my Bible club meeting, Mr. Brown read from the Bible that God put us here to praise him and thank him and give him glory."

"What does it mean to 'give him glory'?" Jennifer wanted to know.

"Well," Jim explained, "if you are honest and kind to people, they will often say, 'That child comes from a good family.' And if people know you belong to God's family, they will be thankful to God for you. That is one way of giving glory to God."

Jim was right. Here is a story about something a boy did that gave glory to his father:

A man lost his billfold with $47 in it. A boy found it. Since the address was in the billfold, the boy took it to the man's house and gave it to him. The man was very glad. He counted the money. All of the $47 was there.

"You are an honest boy," the man said. "Give me your father's name and address because I want to tell him about this. I want to thank him for raising a son like you. He should be very proud of you. You are an honor to your father."

"Thank you," the boy replied. "My dad taught me to love and obey God. I was doing what God would want me to do."

That boy brought praise and glory to his father and to God, his heavenly Father, by the way he acted. Are you doing things that make people want to praise your father and mother and your heavenly Father? I hope so.

A BIBLE VERSE TO READ

O Lord, I will honor and praise your name, for you are my God. You do such wonderful things!

Isaiah 25:1

SOME QUESTIONS TO ANSWER

1. How did a boy bring honor to his father and to his heavenly Father?
2. What are some things you can do to bring honor to your family and to God?

SOME THINGS TO PRAY ABOUT

♦ Thank God for your family and ask him to show you ways to honor them.
♦ Pray that the way you live will always honor God—that you will give him glory.

A Prize for You in Heaven

DO YOU like to win prizes? Maybe you have been in a race at a picnic or at school. Maybe ribbons were given to those who won.

Do you know that there is a prize in heaven that Jesus wants to give you? Now don't ask me what the prize is, because I don't know. It is going to be a surprise—a very wonderful surprise from

God himself. He will give it to you because he loves you so much.

Even though I don't know what the prize is, I can tell you how to get the prize. If you have asked God to forgive your sins, you are part of his family. As God's child, you earn the prize by the good and kind things you do.

So the way you live while you are here on earth is very important. You will live here in this world for only a few short years. Perhaps it seems a long time to think of living until you are 60 or 70 or 80 years old. But it is not very long if you think about how long *forever* is. God's children will be with him in heaven forever.

The prize or reward that God is getting ready for you is one that will last forever. He wants to give you a reward that will make you very happy. How sad it will be if you get to heaven and find that your reward is very small! Then you will wish and wish that you could come back to earth and try for a better prize. But it will be too late.

It is not too late now. You have your whole life ahead of you. You can spend your time doing everything for the Lord Jesus. You can please Jesus when you play, when you go to school, and when you work. You'll be glad if you decide now, when you are still young, to live your life for God. Then, when you get to heaven, how happy you will be!

A BIBLE VERSE TO READ
> See, I am coming soon, and my reward is with me, to repay all according to their deeds.
> *Revelation 22:12*

SOME QUESTIONS TO ANSWER
1. Why will God give you a prize someday?
2. Have you done anything today that would help you have a good prize in heaven?
3. Have you done anything to keep you from getting a prize?

SOME THINGS TO PRAY ABOUT
- ◆ Thank God for letting you be part of his family. (If you haven't already asked him to forgive your sins so you can be in his family, you can do that now.)
- ◆ Thank God for the prize he wants to give you in heaven someday.

About the Author

Kenneth N. Taylor is best known as the writer of *The Living Bible,* which has been revised by a group of biblical scholars to become the New Living Translation. His first claim to fame, though, was as a writer of children's books. Ken and his wife, Margaret, have ten children and 28 grandchildren, so he has personally told many children about God!

It has always been Ken Taylor's desire to make Bible truths easily understandable to everyone. As with this current book, *Family Devotions for Children,* his early books were written to use in families' daily devotions. The early manuscripts were ready for publication only when they passed the scrutiny of ten young critics! Those books, which have been read to two generations of children around the world, include *The Bible in Pictures for Little Eyes* (Moody Press), *Devotions for the Children's Hour* (Moody Press), *The Living Bible Story Book* (Tyndale House), and *Big Thoughts for Little People* (Tyndale House).

Kenneth Taylor continues to have a passion for sharing the gospel with children through his writing. Some of his recent books include *Right Choices, My First Bible Words: A Kid's Devotional* (written with William O. Noller), and *Everything a Child Should Know about God.*

About the Illustrator

Shelley Matheis is a graduate of Montclair State University, Upper Montclair, New Jersey. She has created many illustrations for children's magazines, with her work appearing frequently in *Highlights for Children, Pockets,* and *Cobblestone.*

To create the line art for the interior of *Family Devotions for Children,* this illustrator used pen and ink. Her whimsical drawings capture the thoughts and feelings of the characters described in the devotional readings. For the book's cover she added watercolor washes to create a colorful painting.

Shelley lives in Bloomfield, New Jersey, where she enjoys another creative activity—gardening.